A
Layman's Guide
to
Successful
Publicity

Oscar Leiding

Published by AYER PRESS
210 West Washington Square, Philadelphia, Pa. 19106

AYER PRESS PUBLICATIONS

- Ayer Directory of Publications
- This Is Advertising (ad career guide)
- Ayer Public Relations and Publicity Style Book
- Ayer Glossary of Advertising and Related Terms
- Ayer Fund-Raising Dinner Guide
- A Layman's Guide to Successful Publicity

INTERNATIONAL
STANDARD BOOK NUMBER
0-910190-09-7

TABLE OF CONTENTS

Introduction

Chapters

Sample Releases and Fact Sheets

About the author . . .

Oscar Leiding has had extensive experience in journalism and public relations. Graduated from the University of Illinois, Mr. Leiding went from several newspapers in Illinois to the Associated Press. He was with the AP in Washington, London and New York City. He later joined McGraw-Hill as managing editor of Air Transport Magazine. In 1946 he joined the Public Relations and Publicity Department of N. W. Ayer ABH International, becoming director in 1966.

After retirement from Ayer, he joined The Electrical Distributor Magazine as managing editor, a position he currently holds. Mr. Leiding is a member of the Society of Professional Journalists—Sigma Delta Chi, of which organization he was a national officer for 10 years and president of the New York chapter, The Deadline Club. He is a member of the Public Relations Society of America and of the New York newspapermen's Society of the Silurians.

W. J. Luedke
Publisher

INTRODUCTION

You have been elected, appointed or drafted to handle publicity for an organization in your community.

This organization could be a charity, a men's or women's club, an auxiliary, a church group, a P.T.A., a cultural society, a youth or senior citizens' organization, a fraternal order, a hospital or special health-oriented program, a civic club, a chapter or unit of a national association, or perhaps a small business.

You received the publicity assignment probably not because of a journalism background but because someone believed you could do the job. You have shown the credentials of interest and willingness. As a nonprofessional, you therefore are eager to know how to go about it. This guidebook was written for you.

You have a great honor—and a very great responsibility—because you are a *key* person in the success of your organization.

This is so because the kind and amount of news your community reads or hears about your organization will determine to a great extent what the community will think about it. And what the community thinks about your group and its activities will, in turn, determine how it supports it—whether your need is for more active and interested members, or financial support, or just better understanding and appreciation, the magic quality of goodwill.

If the publicity role is a new one for you, you are fortunate if your predecessor was good at the job, told you about his method of operation, and passed on to you the names of his press contacts, their deadlines, and a clipping book. Such information is invaluable, and will give you a good running start in organizing your program. You can get a running start also if your group is a part of a national organization. Some guidelines usually are available from national headquarters. But the guidelines in this book should enable you to add an extra local dimension to any national guidelines.

In most cases, however, you must start from scratch. And this book is designed to start you from scratch by detailing what you need to know about how to find your outlets, how to work with them, how to write, and even what to do when it appears that there's nothing to write about.

There are no promises of any Pulitzer Prizes (though the principles of news writing given here are no different from those followed by prize winners), but there is the promise of a lot of job satisfaction for you and rewards for your organization.

Every book on news writing emphasizes six elements: Who? What? When? Where? Why? and How? This book also takes as its text the answering of these same questions. The who, as seen in this introduction, is you and your organization. The answers to the other questions follow.

I WHAT PUBLICITY IS— WHY IT'S IMPORTANT

What Is Publicity?

An often-heard slick answer, usually uttered contemptuously, sometimes ignorantly, is that it is "free advertising."

Hard-nosed newspapermen will say this, especially when a local businessman seeks—even demands—space to promote his particular service or product through the news columns by means of stories that are nothing more than gratuitous plugs.

Publicity in this guidebook means *information with news value* issued as a means of gaining public attention, recognition, understanding or support for a person, an organization, an institution or a cause.

The key words that distinguish this kind of publicity from "free advertising" are "information with news value." If you are going to win friends and influence people by publicity through the printed word (newspapers and magazines) and the spoken word (radio and television), you must offer information of public interest. *In other words, news!*

There is no charge, of course, if a publicity release is used. But it really isn't free, if you look at it closely. It has cost the author time to prepare the material and it does cost money to process and deliver releases, plus photography, if that is involved. And, unlike advertising, there is no assurance that it will be published. Moreover, there is no assurance of *what* will be published, if any

3

of it is used. In advertising, of course, you have control over the content of the message and the timing of its placement. And you can repeat the message as often as you can afford to do so.

However, when your publicity is used, in print or over the air, you gain a precious something advertising cannot offer. The message in the story in a newspaper is accepted by readers (and over the air by listeners) as coming from a disinterested third party: the paper or the station . . . not a self-seeking you . . . and therefore tends to have a credibility, a believability, a force that advertising has difficulty matching.

You've often heard the comment, "Last night's paper said . . .," about a news story—but rarely about an advertisement.

Defining publicity another way: We all like to have a favorable image, to be well-liked. The over-all way of developing and maintaining a favorable image, called *public relations,* is doing something good—and *publicity* is telling about it. First, good deeds. Second, good communication.

Why Publicity Is Important

There are a number of reasons why publicity is important to the giver and to the receiver—that is, to your group and to the media.

To Your Group

Your publicity needs may relate to a wide range of nonprofit activities on behalf of community causes carried on virtually everywhere in the nation. There are women's clubs and garden clubs and service clubs; there are churches and groups within churches; there are charities; there are hospitals and health campaigns; there are educational institutions and programs; there are all sorts of youth organizations—athletic, agricultural, scouting, social, anti-drug, etc.; and many others. Here are some of the important benefits of a good publicity program to any of these groups:

- You gain recognition of your good deeds in the community—that is, you develop greater community awareness and goodwill.
- You give your workers the warm glow, the personal satisfaction that what they are doing is noticed, understood, appreciated.
- You help to make your members proud of belonging. (Everyone likes to be associated with a known success.)
- You encourage greater participation by your membership in your activities.
- You heighten your appeal to prospective members— to make them want to belong.
- You develop greater financial support.
- You develop other kinds of support besides time and money, such as free play areas, meeting rooms or donations of goods or equipment.

Let's get specific and take a Cub Scout Pack as an example. Good publicity can provide these benefits:

- Recognition of its members for doing worthwhile things. (Good for morale.)
- Attracting the attention of new recruits. (Membership value.)
- Developing the understanding, the pride and the cooperation of parents. (Winning their greater participation.)
- Positive community action. (Financial support.)

Now you can get specific about your own organization and, by measuring its objectives against these factors, you can see for yourself how publicity can be an essential ingredient in its success—whatever its aims.

5

LAYMAN'S PUBLICITY GUIDE

To the Media

The media comprise newspapers, magazines and other printed publications, such as newsletters, and the so-called broadcast or electronic media—radio and television.

Newspapers are the principal channels for community publicity. There is scarcely a city, town or neighborhood that isn't covered by one or more newspapers. And almost everybody reads them. Surveys show that over eight out of ten households are exposed to one or more newspapers every day. Moreover, while space always is at a premium, newspapers can accommodate a greater quantity of news items.

According to the '76 *Ayer Directory of Publications* there were 1,813 daily newspapers in this country; 8,735 weeklies; and 756 newspapers of other issuing frequencies.

News is their business and here is why your publicity efforts are important to them:

1. The activities of local people and local organizations are news. Publishing it is good business, for local news ranks high in readership, and high readership attracts advertising.
2. Newspaper outside staffs tend to be small. The limited personnel can cover only a few local events, so they must depend upon volunteers—which is what publicity people in essence are—to be their eyes and ears and writers. Without these outside services, local news would dry to a trickle.
3. Newspaper inside staffs also tend to be small. There just is not time under work load and deadline pressures for extensive typing or rewriting of the material that must be processed to fill an edition. Hence, if you can contribute a publicity release that has news interest and has been prepared in a professional manner, you help the harried editor.

4. Newspapers appreciate ideas as well as copy. And who should know better what constitutes a good news feature idea about a person or an organization than a publicity man or woman thoroughly familiar with the organization and its personnel?

None of this, however, should mislead you into believing that getting publicity is as easy as rolling off a log and that you will be welcomed with open arms in every newspaper city room. Sometimes yes; sometimes no!

Newspaper space is limited, and the competition for it is fierce. There is world news, there is national news, there is state news, and there is regional and local news in staggering quantities. Heap onto that a large number of deserving local nonprofit organizations clamoring for attention. And there's still more! The business enterprises important to the economy of the community also seek attention.

Wading through all this on a daily newspaper is a tremendous chore. A weekly is spared the world and national news, but it gets its full share of the rest. Small wonder, then, that an editor's attitude toward borderline publicity will be chilly and to his time-wasters, explosive. He has room for so little—on a daily, let's say something less than 10 percent of what comes in.

But do not despair. As you should not be misled into believing that getting publicity is easy, you should not now be misled into believing that getting it is hopeless or impossible. Not if it is interesting to readers and well prepared.

Recognize the extreme competition for space. Be aware of the editorial pressures. Then go to work in the knowledge that a flow of good local news is a newspaper necessity and confident that, if you make positive contributions to that flow, you will win editorial respect and have success in your publicity assignment.

You will realize that your success will be doubly rewarding. Your efforts will enable the press to better meet its responsibility to provide readers with timely and interesting information. And at the same time you'll be helping your organization to build its community image.

Next is a detailed answer to your likely question: "Where do I begin?"

II   WHERE TO BEGIN

As the new publicity chairman, you have two places where you should begin to set up an effective program:

    I. In your organization
    II. With the media

Here are action plans for each of these areas.

I—In Your Organization

Just as a salesman must know his product before going out to sell, it is imperative that you know what news-generating activities there are in your organization.

If your predecessor is available, start with him or her to learn what was done in the past. If a clipping book has been kept, study it carefully.

But let's assume you must start from scratch. Here is a listing of steps to be taken:

1. Familiarize yourself with the over-all objectives of your organization. You must know its basic aims to be able to decide on what audiences to focus your publicity efforts. What are the functions and what are the goals? Is fund raising a major objective or is community prestige the principal aim? Read the charter and by-laws or articles of incorporation as well as other official documents. If there is a history, read it and maybe read it again. If your organization is a part of a larger body, get all the background you can from headquarters.

2. Get a calendar of activities and events (or make up your own, if you have to) and sit down with the head of your organization and the program chairman to review it in detail. If there are holes in the program, keep your eyes open as you settle into your job; you may have suggestions for filling them later.

3. The basic aims you already know, but find out from the head of your organization and other officers and committee members what special immediate objectives there may be and what particular problems are pressing. Is a new-member drive being considered? Is greater member participation a critical problem? Is an infusion of young blood needed? Increased financial support? Greater community involvement? Are plans being developed to attack these problems, and how soon will they be completed?

4. Get an up-to-date list of officers, committees and, if available, a complete roster of members. By all means, you must have the addresses, telephone numbers and professional titles, if pertinent, of all officers and committee members.

5. Establish some working rules with your group's head. You should be your organization's only contact with the press—for multiple contacts are confusing. But if there are special reasons for another contact—and they must be very special—who is this contact and how will the joint effort be coordinated? If you are the sole contact, determine who will serve when you are unavailable. You'll want to establish also whether your publicity releases will have to be cleared with anyone. If so, with whom?

6. Find out if there is a publicity budget. If there is none, but the practice has been to be reimbursed for postage, photography and other ordinary out-of-pocket expenses from other funds, find out how much was spent in, say, the preceding year.

If there is no publicity budget, and no past practice of reimbursement, make the point that there are necessary expenses and that you will recommend a budget as soon as you have a better grasp of the dimensions of your over-all program. Stationery and other office supplies may be available from your organization; otherwise they should be a part of your budget.

It should be noted that the Internal Revenue Service allows you to deduct out-of-pocket expenses, such as gasoline and oil, when you do volunteer work for a *charitable* organization. Instead of figuring what you spent for gas and oil, you can take a straight mileage allowance. Since IRS rules change from time to time, you'll want to check the latest income tax regulations for current allowances, and be sure to keep a running record of your mileage. You cannot, of course, deduct any amount for which you were reimbursed.

7. Skip ahead to the next section of this chapter to determine the kinds of information the media in your area will use, and when you have done what it suggests, come back here. In the light of this media knowledge, and your knowledge of what your organization has to offer, sketch out a working publicity program—what you propose to do and when you propose to do it. This will be your blueprint and timetable for action.

8. Review your blueprint and timetable with the head of your organization and the program chairman. Be candid with yourself—and have your associates understand that when *routine* meetings are held, there will be no publicity or, at best, only routine publicity. To be interesting to a broad audience, your organization must engage in events and activities that have obvious community value. If it is clear that the events and activities do not promise much news interest, you can brace your colleagues in advance against high expectations. If they want to remedy that lack by strengthen-

ing the organization's program with special projects and new activities, that will be another matter on which a study of the "What-to-Write Checklist" in Chapter III could be a convenient starting point.

9. Prepare a fact sheet that you can send to the press, or leave when you call, as a background document for their reference files. It should give your name as publicity contact, your telephone number, your address, and the same information for any alternative contact. If you are at one place during certain hours and at another the rest of the time, give both telephone numbers and the hours when available at each. Also list your officers, again with telephone numbers and addresses, and give your committee roster. Double-check all information to be certain it is accurate.

The fact sheet should include highlights of your organization's history—when it was founded; over-all objectives; significant events; honors won, etc. Prepare it with three uses in mind—an editor's use if he needs something quickly to add background to a story; your own use in preparing publicity releases; and use by any speakers who may be talking about your organization. (See Sample Fact Sheet No. 1 on page 156.)

II—With the Media

How many times have you said, "There's nothing in the paper tonight!"? Or heard it said by someone else? Of course there's something in the paper. It's full of news and features. But sometimes there is more of interest to you than other times.

Part of your problem as publicity chairman will be to see to it that what you write is interesting to others. Do your level best to make it bright and worthwhile. Pledge to yourself to shun the dull; don't contribute to the material that will make others say: "There's nothing in the paper tonight."

Keep this pledge in mind as you proceed along the following paths given in one-two fashion, though not necessarily to be followed strictly in order:

1. Build Your Media List

Of course, the newspaper boy faithfully makes his daily deliveries to your door and the mailman stuffs the box with the local weekly, the shopper giveaway, and perhaps a regional news-feature weekly.

But are these *all* the publications you should know about for your publicity program? Undoubtedly not. You need to make up a *complete master list*.

A good way to compile a master list is to go to your public library and check the *Ayer Directory of Publications* for the names of all publications serving the area your publicity should reach. Start with your own community and jot down the publication names, addresses and telephone numbers.

Then look up all the surrounding communities whose publications also may circulate where your organization operates. It may be that the next town north of you may be of no consequence in your scheme of things, but the newspapers east and west may have good readership in your community. But, for the moment, jot them all down because, in due course, you will want to look at them all and judge the potential interest in your publicity for yourself.

Your list may include local and nearby daily newspapers, weeklies, semiweeklies, and shopper weeklies. Then extend your range to the big-city newspapers that circulate in your area, some of which may have special suburban news sections publishing the kind of material you will be developing. Also, check for regional news-feature publications (some weeklies, some monthlies) that may circulate in your community.

If you are in a large city, your outlets will be limited—but list them all anyway. Concentrate on any community publication your part of the city may have; check the big dailies for early-edition community sections; but otherwise don't worry about them until you come up with something unusual or spectacular.

Up to this point, nothing has been said about radio and television because, as pointed out in Chapter I, newspapers are the principal channels for community publicity. Hence, the emphasis first on them and on news-feature type regional publications.

However, while you're at the library, at least check on the availability of radio-television directories. If one is available, make a list of the stations. If none is available, you might try the nearest big-city library, an advertising agency, or go directly to a broadcast station.

2. Analyze Your Outlets

Your next step will be to look through all the publications you have written down on your master list.

What you want to learn, very simply, is: "Will *my* stories be news to the readers of these newspapers?"

So, see for yourself by studying each newspaper closely as to

- the kinds of stories each editor likes
- how the stories are written
- what kinds of pictures are used
- whether there is a certain day each week when a daily has a special column, or page, or section for a particular kind of community activity.

A newspaper in a large city may offer little or no opportunity for your news. Or, a newspaper on one side of your city may carry no news at all about your community's activities, while another, perhaps even farther away, may carry quite a bit.

What you want to do is concentrate your efforts where they will count. Discard the no-no's; put the borderline ones on the fringe; but aim your shots at the real targets.

While you are at your library, you may find that it has its reading room well stocked with area publications. If so, your job of surveying the field will be easier.

Otherwise, beg, borrow, or buy the publications on your master list, and study them carefully *over a period.* Reading them over an extended period of time will indicate whether there is some day each week when a daily gives space to a certain activity, and whether any seasonal patterns are observable. If so, you'll want to relate such patterns to your own responsibility.

It is a good idea to start a folder for each publication that may be an outlet for your work. Make notes on the coverage it gives to your type of activity. Clip some stories, if you can (though not at the library), to tuck away as good examples that you can use for ideas or models.

3. Get Acquainted

Now you should be ready to get to know the people with the media—not only to get to know them, but also to let them get to know you.

There are many good reasons for making personal calls:

- To build the editor's knowledge, confidence and respect for you as a news source, thus increasing receptivity for your material.
- To give the editor a specific point of contact whom he knows personally when he needs more information about your organization.

- To give you some very important working tools.

In this latter category, you will find the following information most helpful:

Deadlines. Establish the deadlines for each of the kinds of stories you expect to produce—deadlines for the routine, deadlines for the exceptional, deadlines for the unusual emergency. And deadlines for photographs as well as news. Find out not only what the regular deadlines are, but what they are for holiday periods. A weekly that "goes to bed" on a particular day each ordinary week will have a different deadline for, say, the Thanksgiving weekend.

Contacts. Determine how to address your material—to an editor by name, or to a desk (the city desk) or to a department.

Format. How does a publication prefer to see the incoming information presented? Almost all will accept double-spaced typing, but there are a few that prefer triple spacing. Whatever other special preferences may exist should be understood. (Helpful information relating to format and contacts can be found in sections #1 and #2 of the *Ayer Public Relations and Publicity Style Book.*)

Emergencies. You should know when not to call with a routine question—but what about an unusual situation—a top-drawer news break? Whether it is something in your organization or something you have witnessed, find out what to do. It won't hurt you in your job, for example, to call about some spot news event you have witnessed. In fact doing so should help to build rapport!

Programmed Events. Does a paper want a phone call in advance about something good—but programmed—coming up? Or is the usual calendar sufficient to make an editor want only quick coverage after an event?

Special Coverage. Does a paper outside your community have a special reporter or writer assigned to visit your community periodically? If so, when and where can you reach this person; what is his special responsibility; is he at the newspaper, or available in your community?

Live Coverage. When does the editor like to have a reporter at a function of your organization? Usually he will depend upon you, because of staff limitations, but what are the exceptions?

Special Interests. A reporter usually is very busy in his job. But he may live in your community and have a special interest in your organization. Find out what his interests are, and also those of his family.

Unless you have a predecessor to guide you, make an advance telephone call to the editorial department and ask who it is you should see and the most convenient time to come in to get acquainted. Close to edition time is *not* the time to go. Everyone is too busy. Go when you are welcome—and keep your visit as brief as possible.

If you have a story to offer, bring it with you and use it as a point of discussion. If you have a fact sheet on your organization (a project recommended earlier), go over it briefly and leave a copy. Then get into the questions of deadlines and the other information already listed among the purposes of your call.

Leave with your contact your name, address and telephone number, either as a part of your fact sheet, or by itself if you have no fact sheet, and the name of your organization. This is for the newspaper's reference file.

On the receiving end, you should jot down the names and titles of your new contact and any of his colleagues he may suggest as important to your assignment. Establish how to reach them.

For mailed material, get an exact address; for delivered material, get not only the right address, but note any special situations—such as how to get stories to the night staff of an afternoon newspaper when the usual doors may be locked.

Editors, of course, are very busy people. If you call on the telephone to make an appointment and are told a personal visit is not necessary, find out to whom you should talk. Then, when you have reached this contact, give a quick summary of your organization and the information you can provide. Ask some of the key questions—deadlines, etc.—you would ask on a personal visit. Since you can't cover the ground completely, get as much information as you need to get started; then drop a note to your contact saying that you look forward to working with him and asking for the opportunity to call him again on any points you were not able to cover in the first brief call.

III   WHAT TO WRITE

To answer the question of what to write, start by putting yourself into the shoes of a news editor. He's your target. The more you help him do *his* job, the better your success in *your* job.

What is his job? It is to capture and hold the attention of his audience (whether readers or listeners or viewers) by his selection of:

1. Current events and
2. Features—that will *interest* and *inform*.

Thus, what you should write is *interesting information.*

And the broader the audience that you can inform and interest, the greater the likelihood that your publicity will be used. Very simply, if you deliver what the news editor needs to do a good job, he'll use it.

But what is interesting information? What qualifies? And what goes into the wastebasket? (Remember, the volume of flow is such that he has to pitch away perhaps 90 percent of what he receives!)

For answers, start by putting yourself back into your own shoes as a reader and answer for yourself what interests *you* in a newspaper, in a magazine, or in a newscast. Now, multiply this one *you* by all the persons you know, and know about, and you'll have some good ideas on what to write.

Of course, if your organization has a strong program of activities that have been making news, the answer to the question of what to write is very simple: just plunge right in and go to work with what you have. The news that was made in the past should provide examples for you to follow.

Even if you have numerous examples to follow, there will be many opportunities for further visibility that just have not been explored. You will want to improve upon what your predecessor did. So there may be some nuggets for you to mine in the listing that follows.

On the other hand, if your organization has not had a past pattern of publicity success, you'll get some ideas of your own after the talks you'll have within your organization and with newspaper editors.

In either case, you may have the feeling that it all needs to be put into focus. This gets us back to simply addressing the question of what to write.

You should start by sorting out the things you can write about for your organization under the two great areas of the news editor's interest—current events and features.

I—What Are Current Events?

In *current events,* the key or operative word is *current.*

The information you prepare in this category must interest it must inform but it also *must be timely.* The time element is all-important. Something is going to happen, soon. Or something did happen, today, last night, last week. It is *news.*

Let's suppose your organization concentrates on only one major annual event, say, a top-drawer banquet, an open house, an international picnic. What is there for you to write? The answer comes down to (1) advane releases announcing that something is going to happen and (2) an after-the-event report on what did happen.

Advance releases are a valuable part of your publicity program because they will help promote support for your event. But when and how many?

Here again, timeliness is an important factor. An advance release in March on a picnic to be held in August hardly qualifies as timely—even though the decision to hold the picnic came in March. In general, the closer to the date, the stronger the news appeal of an advance announcement.

As to how many, that depends upon how often you have something worthwhile to report. A reminder announcement once a month for two or three months in advance of an event won't get you newspaper space if it's nothing more than the same old announcement over and over again. But if you can develop a succession of fresh announcements of public interest, you can have your project publicized repeatedly.

For example, if the gala event your group is staging is a major event for your community, not just for your organization, an advance release program might include an announcement of the naming of the project chairman; perhaps the naming of a working committee; a progress report if material and interest justify; and later, the announcement of a top speaker or other major program development. Then, close to the date itself, a round-up advance release with all the details.

In most cases, however, the news in your organization probably will not justify such an ambitious program. The annual election of officers, for example, usually will not call for any advance announcement. But it will call for an after-the-event release, possibly with a photograph of the president or a group photograph.

Yet, no matter what it calls for, the information *must be timely*. If you can deliver a release to a daily newspaper reporting something that happened "today" or "yesterday," or to a weekly reporting something that happened "this week" or "last weekend," you'll be accenting that it is news and you'll enhance your chances of getting it into print.

Thus, what you should write under this current event or news category is *interesting and timely information.*

To develop a working program, go through the activities calendar of your organization and pick out all the events that have dates—that qualify on the basis of a time element for consideration as news. Then give them an interest ranking—the major events that may lend themselves to a series of advance announcements; the events that will deserve only after-they're-over reports; and the standard meeting schedules of interest only to your members.

Routine information, such as the latter, can best be communicated by postcard, newsletter, a phone brigade, or other means. While you should be candid with yourself, and try not to bother newspapers with the routine, nevertheless you should find out what to do to announce a cancellation forced by an emergency. If heavy snow, a bad sleet storm, sudden flooding or other unexpected event forces a cancellation, you should know where to call to get the word out. A newspaper may set up an "emergency information desk" and it will, if it is connected with a radio station, get the news to the station for broadcast. Or, you may call your area's radio stations yourself to give the news. In such times as these, however, manpower is limited and calls to regular numbers may not get through. So it is wise to check in advance as to what your procedure should be in time of emergency.

While routine meetings may get little or no space as individual news items—and your study of the publications will show you what you can expect—many newspapers publish special calendars of community activities. If so, just find out the deadline—usually earlier than for spot news—and send in any announcements that qualify. Don't waste your time (or the editor's) trying to get more than such a listing for the routine.

II—What Is A Feature?

Features are the second great domain of interest to editors— and a most rewarding field for a publicity program carried out with imagination, some extra thought, some good ideas, some extra effort.

In some cases, where the news in an organization is largely routine, the feature is the *only* way to gain interest and attention. Where there is a good flow of news, the feature provides an exciting *extra dimension*. Moreover, the feature is the *only* type of material used by some publications, notably regional newspaper-type magazines or standard format regional magazines.

Before any definitions of a feature, let's take an example from the world of sports that even non-sports-minded people should find descriptive:

In 1973 as Henry (Hank) Aaron was closing in on Babe Ruth's career home-run mark of 714, each home run he hit was *news*. (That gets us back to the category covered in the preceding section of this chapter: News. Something happening *now* . . . *to-day* . . . TODAY! NEWS!)

But when the 1973 season ended, Aaron was one home run shy of tying Ruth's record. News-wise, no more news on the race until 1974 (unless something happened to Aaron).

But, feature-wise, all sorts of angles to be explored during the off-season by inquisitive, imaginative, interest-oriented news-papermen, magazine writers, broadcasters and publicity people.

So, some enterprising person zeroed in on the bats . . . and the story came forth that the same bat factory that produced Ruth's bats furnished Aaron with his.

This made a story—with a lot of newspaper space about the details of the bats, the similarities and the differences, etc. It was a story because it was interesting to an audience; secondly, a timeless story in the sense that it did not have the "today" of spot news; and, finally, that it was timely because it dealt with a situation during a period of current interest.

An editor might say: "Good today, tomorrow, next week, next month. I can use it any time I have the space—or need an interesting feature—up to the time Hank Aaron hits number 714. But, even then, all this background information—interesting to sports buffs—can be used again when number 714 is hit; or when number 715 is hit (a new record); or at any time thereafter."

Again, what is a feature?

Like a news story, it's a story that must be interesting—but unlike a news story it does not have the urgency of a today or yesterday or tomorrow angle.

But a feature usually has some timeliness (as the story of Hank Aaron's bat had a seasonal timeliness) or it can even be one without any relation to time, such as a background story on the fact that the president of your organization writes children's verse in her spare time.

In short, the point of interest does not usually come from the immediacy of an event—as it does in a news story—but from some other element.

One such element is *human interest*. A story on your president writing children's verse would be based on human interest.

Another such element is *history*. An anniversary story presenting the colorful history of your organization's beginnings is an example. The big dinner celebrating the anniversary calls for a news story—but a background feature in advance of that celebration will be very much in order if there is interesting detail. Anniversary features can be about an organization, or people, or buildings, or products, or events.

Another such element might be the peculiar accident that

caused something to happen—something along the truth-is-stranger-than fiction approach. How a chance idea of a person in a group sparked the beginning of your organization, might serve as a feature platform.

When you watch a television news program, you see a certain amount of spot news coverage—an event in Washington or your state capital or in your community; a bad accident, a report on the weather; a segment on sports. But you also see *features*—the travels of Charles Couralt on CBS is an example. Similarly, you will see many articles in the newspapers you read that are not spot news but are "timely-timeless" articles of interest.

Features call for a bit of imagination because they do not derive their interest purely from the fact that something happened or is going to happen. Reporting an event calls for the skills of accuracy, brevity and good observation—but a feature requires a bit of ingenuity, a colorful pen, sometimes a sense of drama, occasionally a sense of humor, and always a sense of what's interesting.

There are features to be developed in every organization and, in many cases, they will be the most interesting things you will do. The news is important—but it can be humdrum—and it may win you a small bit of space. Where your efforts really will pay off very often—both in your own "job satisfaction" and in the extra visibility you will gain for your organization—is in the field of features.

So, in this end of your assignment, dig as deeply as you can into the history of your organization. Dig into the backgrounds of its people. If there are archives, take the time to go through them thoroughly. Make notes of dates—dates of events, birthdays of people, dates of buildings—for anniversary possibilities, both for feature stories and news. If there are no archives, interview all the people you can—particularly the older members and also those who may be inactive now but were influential earlier. Check the newspaper morgues (libraries) and your historical society, if there is one, and any other source you hear about. It will be fun exploring—and you may find a lot of answers to the question of what to write that no one in your organization ever found before.

In specific reply to the question of what to write, here is a list of opportunities for news and features. Some of them may already exist in your organization, others can and perhaps should be developed for an effective publicity program.

What-to-Write Checklist

Achievement

Recognizing achievement is one of the surest ways of gaining editorial attention. Awards, as explained under "Awards," gain attention—but they are only one of several devices for recognizing achievement.

If your organization doesn't give a scholarship, or a medal, or a cup, it still can command news and feature coverage if it honors achievement some other way. Perhaps it selects the "Gardener of the Year," or the "Citizen of the Year," or the "Community Woman of the Year," or "The Athlete of the Week," or the "Mayor-for-a-Day," the announcement of recognition being the honor. (See sample release on page 138.)

More distinction can be added to the achievement recognition by making it an occasion for a special luncheon, or dinner, or banquet.

Sometimes a member of your organization may be the recipient of a special honor in his profession. You are not giving him an award—but you want to tip your organization's hat in congratulation and recognition. You should do so by writing a news story or feature.

Thus, you'll want to look for opportunities to recognize an individual for merit, for unusual achievement, or for contribution in whatever world he serves—whether he's an 8-year-old Cub Scout or the Chairman of the Board.

Actions

Any action of your organization that has community interest should be a subject for your typewriter. This could be a committee vote on a matter that affects the community as a whole; it could be a new policy or procedure of outside interest; or it could be taking a stand on an issue of great local importance. With today's accent on ecology, the environment and conservation, a youth drive to collect wastepaper and bottles, or a garden club's decision to buy and preserve a wetlands area would be examples of newsworthy actions. (See sample releases on pages 141 and 148.)

Anniversaries

These offer good opportunities for both news and features. An anniversary can be an every-year news event—the annual banquet with an important speaker, the annual award—perhaps the *only* news event on your organization's calendar. Or an anniversary can be a very special event when it is the 10th, or 25th, or 50th, 75th or 100th birthday. (See sample releases on pages 145 and 148 and Sample Fact Sheet No. 2 on page 158.) Anniversaries can be celebrations of milestones in an organization's history; or of people (your founder, your president, anyone important to your beginning or your development); or of buildings; or projects; or of service (such as the 20th anniversary of the first book sent abroad by Book Aid). If you belong to a national organization, its anniversaries can be locally observed, but your own anniversaries also are important—for example, the 25th or 50th anniversary of the Boy Scout movement locally, which doesn't coincide with any national anniversary.

The point is that anniversaries offer natural occasions on which to capitalize. They invite you to look—and look very carefully and very imaginatively—at what *you* can do and what you can encourage others to do to exploit them to advantage. If there are celebrations, that is news. But even when there are no celebrations there are interesting features that can be written that editors will use.

Appointments

Appointments make news because appointments are names. In addition, they often mean action—something happening or about to happen. They mean action when the appointment is to a special project. Addresses as well as names should be given in your news stories for newspapers using addresses; also give business connections, if appropriate.

Appointments may be made to committees, to special projects, to special functions. In any case, they are news because they are names—and they could be features if a project or a name so warrants. (See sample releases on pages 151 and 155.)

Awards

There is nothing simpler or easier for gaining news attention than giving an award. The announcement of an award is news, and the formal presentation may be news. If an award is an annual one, it gets extra attention on the special anniversaries—10th, 20th, 25th, 50th, etc. Then, particularly, you may be able to develop features—tracing the careers of the early recipients as well as developing the history of the award. Look closely at what the award really means—and fan out from there.

In this category, the emblems of honor are legion— a scholarship . . . an achievement scroll . . . a medal . . . a plaque . . . a trophy . . . a portrait . . . a ribbon . . . a citation. Sometimes an organization honors outsiders, sometimes its own. If your group has no award program, look at least for opportunities to make an occasion out of a service anniversary of one of your leaders. A citation will enhance news attention. (See sample release on pages 131 and 138.)

Banquets

There are regular occasions and special occasions—and a banquet may be associated with either. A banquet in itself isn't a news event, but it becomes one if it is invested with community interest. A father-and-son football banquet, for example, has more natural interest than the annual installation of officers of a small lodge. If a top-drawer award is given at a banquet, or there is a speech by an important person on a topic of community interest, news will be made. Feature interest may be attracted by unusual staging—such as a gourmet dinner cooked by the men, or a garden club banquet featuring a complete menu of exotic produce grown at home. (See sample releases on pages 145 and 148.)

Benefits

As there are so many special benefits, you must be careful here. Your cause may be good, but the competition is fierce. Sit down and analyze carefully and realistically what your organization expects and what it may get. Assuming that you have a Grade A special benefit—a special cause that has great support—go to town with your editors. If your project, on the other hand, appears somewhat marginal to you, discuss it with them candidly. They will advise you what to do. (See sample release on page 153.)

Civic Activities

What contributions does your organization make to the community in general or to special areas—such as education, church, youth, senior citizens, minority groups, handicapped, etc.? Make a list. The nature and amount of the activities will indicate what you can do, publicity-wise, and what you can expect in results. (See sample releases on pages 129, 141 and 148.) If some of what is done is done in association with other groups, get acquainted with their publicity people and provide them with the materials of information they can use to ensure your organization's proper share of exposure. (See also "Community Service.")

Committees

Here is a fertile field for news—assuming, of course, that your committees are active. Committee elections (perhaps an annual procedure) are news. The organization of a new committee could be news; certainly the naming of the members of a new committee, and their assignment, is news. Changes in an important committee will call for a story. Committee reports should be studied; usually there will be no outside interest in them, but when there is, put out a release. (See sample releases on pages 136, 151 and 155.)

Community Service

There is so much in this area that applies to a community organization that it would be difficult to be specific on what things to look for. In some groups, the entire program is dedicated to community service and therefore every element may have some degree of newsworthiness. In others, there may be only a single project, and whether it is major or minor will dictate what you can do. (See sample releases on pages 129, 130, 141, 148 and 153.) Essentially, as outlined under "Civic Activities," contributions to any community group or effort should be worth publicizing.

Look, however, to make two special efforts:

1. If there is a community emergency—a flood, a devastating ice storm, tornado or hurricane, a bad fire—and your organization rises to the occasion with some special service, tell about it. Get the facts and move fast to get them to the news desk. If you can provide photographs quickly, do so.

2. Sometimes a good project runs along year after year as a part of the regular program, solid but unexciting. It is

overlooked because it is taken for granted, or it is ignored because it is "old hat." If it is a worthy program, people should be reminded of it . . . and part of your job should be to find ways to do so. An anniversary approach is a good one here ("For the 20th year in succession, the XYZ Club . . . etc."); or the big-figure approach ("The one-millionth bandage rolled by Circle 7 . . . etc."); or some unusual circumstance may invest the routine with a touch of glamour. With ingenuity, you can rescue an undistinguished project from the shadows.

Conventions

When your organization holds a convention, you have a major publicity undertaking. In such a circumstance it has to be assumed that you are with a large organization with a headquarters staff—and that you will get a lot of guidance from headquarters.

The usual convention involvement is the selection of a delegate or delegation to represent the local group at a regional, state, national or international conclave. (See sample release on page 140.) The nature of the news opportunity will depend upon the importance of the convention. The news value will be greater if the delegate is empowered to vote on an issue of local community interest. There is news interest if a member of your group has a committee responsibility at the convention, and even greater interest if the member is on the program to make a speech.

And don't overlook a report on the return. A Boy Scout's "convention" is the Jamboree—and if a Scout comes back with an interesting photo of himself trading one of your community's products for a souvenir from a far-off land, an editor might use it. Similarly, delegates to a professional or business convention may bring back something of feature interest or news importance. Too many people travel these days, however, both for business and pleasure, for anything but genuine news or an unusual feature to get editorial attention.

Competitions and Contests

These may vary from team competitions (as in sports and bridge) to contests for individuals (as an art competition or an essay contest) and each calls for its own news and feature approaches.

Any kind of sports competition in which your group engages must be covered according to the form and style prescribed by the sports editor of each publication serving your community. Read the sports pages, then have a discussion with each sports editor to determine exactly what he wants, when he wants it, and how he wants it. (As a caution, sports stories often are written in jargon which in some cases is effective but more often is poor and lazy writing. Don't try to imitate a bad example; tell your story straight.)

Bridge, if it is handled at all, is handled in another department—sometimes in the regular news pages, sometimes in the women's pages. If bridge is on your program, it won't rank high for publicity, however, unless it is an unusual competition with a tangible community benefit, or has something else to commend it. But find out from your newspaper contacts what their interest is.

Contests open to individuals call for detailed advance planning of the entire project, and publicity moves along step-by-step as an integral part of it as it unfolds—opening announcement, defining eligibility, the rules and purpose; the naming of the judges; a reminder as the deadline for entries nears; the actual event, if it is an art competition or other public display project; announcement of the winners; formal awarding of the prizes.

Again, seek guidance from your editorial friends. Art especially is a specialized world and it would pay you to discuss an art competition thoroughly in advance with those responsible for art sections.

Dedications

See under "New Facilities."

Demonstrations

Public demonstrations are good publicity material. Since the purpose is to attract spectators, advance news stories are more important than after-the-fact coverage. (See sample release on page 137.)

Drives

There are many different kinds of drives, and some are listed separately (see "Membership Drives" and "Fund Raising"). The publicity potential in a drive depends upon its community interest. Candidly weigh a drive's importance to the public; if it is marginal, take it easy.

Education

Any project in the educational field should be coordinated with the school authorities involved so that publicity assignments are carried out by those best qualified to do so. Work out a cooperative program to take advantage of the assets of both parties. Make sure that you provide the school with all the information about your group's involvement it should have for any publicity it undertakes. (See sample releases on pages 125, 126, 128 and 131.)

Elections

The election of new officers calls for an announcement story giving the names, offices, home addresses, and business affiliations, if appropriate. If an officer of long service is reelected, make special mention of the length of service. The formal installation may also be a news story, with or without photographs, including any recognition of the outgoing officers. (See sample release on page 136.)

LAYMAN'S PUBLICITY GUIDE

Exhibits

An exhibit open to the public is good publicity material. An exhibit might be a part of an anniversary observance, and hence could provide the material for a historical feature. If it is an impressive exhibit, it could call for a formal opening ceremony with a dignitary. Some exhibits will lend themselves better than others to photographs, but photographs should be a part of your publicity. (See sample release on page 150.)

Fund Raising

Fund raising for big dollars or major building programs is a special and highly organized effort usually directed by skilled professionals. Your function often will be only to cooperate in the initial stages by providing all possible information. Later, as the professionals phase out, you can expect to do more and more in carrying out the program, but they will leave a blueprint for you to follow.

Other fund-raising efforts are more modest, and the amount of publicity you can expect will depend on the nature of the cause and the imagination behind the drive. (See sample release on page 153.) Coming up with a new idea could make the difference between news visibility or no press. The same old cookie sale year after year is less inspiring than an enterprising Scout troop buying a ton of bird seed, packaging it in five-pound bags, and peddling it from door to door when the snow has just blanketed the ground. (You'll find a detailed treatment of the subject of fund raising in the *Ayer Fund-Raising Dinner Guide.*)

Honors

Honors may be won or awarded by an organization, or they may be won by individuals within the organization. See "Achievement" and "Awards."

Localizing

Always localize a national or regional news development, if you can. For example, a national organization—the one to which your group belongs—announces a significant new program. Have your president, or executive committee, interpret what this means locally and what your local group intends to do. Suppose you have a special reclamation program and something happens or is said in Washington that points up what you are trying to do. Get out a local statement—and the quicker the better. Interpreting something from outside in terms of your local community's needs or interests always is a good technique. But watch out for controversial subjects—unless your group thrives on controversy.

Membership

News interest in a membership drive depends on the strength of community interest. Where public interest is high, a complete program should be mapped out in advance for the publicity and carried out step by step just as for any other major project.

Membership growth offers a number of story possibilities. One is the achievement of a significant new record. Another is the attainment of a round number—the 100th, the 1,000th, etc.

Meetings

Routine meetings are not worth covering but, as said elsewhere, advance notices should be sent to those newspapers which publish calendars of community activities. Meetings do generate news, however, when officers are elected, committees are appointed, actions are taken on programs or projects, etc. Anything that appears to have public interest should be considered for a story.

New Facilities

New construction . . . expansion . . . modernization . . . moving to new quarters—any one of these contains a great many news opportunities.

To illustrate, here is the range of story opportunities on a new construction project: a story on *why*, pointing up the growth of the organization and its plans for the future; stories on the design—illustrated with architect's concepts—when it comes off the drawing board and is approved; letting the contract; ceremonial ground-breaking; building progress as significant stages are completed; cornerstone laying; dedication; and open house. A whole program of publicity to keep you busy over a long period. Any time an organization builds, expands, modernizes, or moves, it's news—and the bigger the project, the greater the potential. (See sample release on page 143.)

Plans and Programs

If the planning for a year calls for new programs of public interest, these should be announced when adopted and then followed up individually on their merits as they are carried out. The completion of a program also may be newsworthy, being a success story that enhances the organization's image because it reflects credit for a mission completed.

Projects—New and Old

There is news in old projects that continue, year after year, although a fresh approach often needs to be considered to instill new interest. New projects are news because they are new, and present no problem.

Among the projects that have a good measure of built-in public interest, here is a short list:

Special Meetings
Conferences
Forums
Roundtables
Seminars

Shows
Antique shows
Fashion shows
Flower shows
Garden shows
Hobby shows

Open Houses and Tours
Open houses
Headquarters tours
Garden tours
House tours
Office tours

Reports

Some organizations prepare annual reports, which should be studied for public interest. Many annual reports, however, are interesting only to the members.

Progress reports offer possibilities—when a significant milestone has been reached on the way in a drive or on a program.

Social Functions

A reception, a dance, a ball—none of these has news potential if the purpose is purely social. If a ball is a charity affair, however, or offers some other reason for community interest, it should be publicized.

LAYMAN'S PUBLICITY GUIDE

Special Observances

The calendar is full of special days and weeks and months—and any time their celebration is in your group's area of interest you have a ready-made publicity vehicle. Go to your library and find out what references it has that give these special observances. News almanacs usually have a listing, but Congress adds new ones every now and then. Find out, too, about special observances in your own state. And keep alert for anything new proclaimed within your own community. You may even be able to arrange a local proclamation for your own group. Go over your list with your group's officers and decide what applies. Then publicize the local observance of the occasion. (See sample release on page 139.)

Speeches

Speeches are worth news releases if an important announcement is made (see sample release on page 148) or if a distinguished outside speaker is on the rostrum whose presence alone attracts attention. In the latter case, in addition to preparing a release presenting what you believe to be important, prepare an abstract giving highlights of the talk. The abstract will be valuable to pass out if the event attracts any reporters. Moreover, it will be a good accompaniment for your release if a paper depends upon your coverage.

Statements

Statements by your president or executive committee may be issued announcing a stand on a public question of national or local importance. See "Localizing."

Surveys

A popular way of making news is to conduct a survey. Any survey constituting a representative sampling on a subject of local interest, and within your group's scope of operations, is worth publicizing.

Unusual Subjects or Events

Editors thrive on the unusual—so seek constantly to uncover and to write about the unusual. Unusual service . . . unusual performance . . . unusual hobbies—these are some of the things that will make good copy.

VIP's

A distinguished visitor may make news for your group just by visiting it or the news may be made by an action (ground-breaking for a new building, for example) or by a speech. Depending on the time and the visitor's role, you may want to organize a press conference. First check, however, to see that the visitor approves. If a conference is held, have for the press a short fact sheet giving background on the visitor and the purpose of the local visit. Arrange for pictures to be taken with your president and other officers. For coverage of a speech, see "Speeches."

IV

HOW TO WRITE PUBLICITY

Here is a recipe for good news writing that will tell you in one sentence all you need to know about how to write publicity:

"Put it before them briefly so they will read it, clearly so they will appreciate it, picturesquely so they will remember it and, above all, accurately so they will be guided by its light."

Follow those words of Joseph Pulitzer, the famous publisher and founder of the Pulitzer prizes, and you will delight the editors with your contributions and your organization with your results.

For you to put this recipe to work, step-by-step procedures follow:

New Stories

1. Begin by gathering every bit of information you can on the event you are going to write up. If there are names, get them accurately. Make sure that you have correct titles and addresses. Assemble every scrap of detail possible; it is easy to throw away what you don't need.

2. As acknowledged earlier, a good news story will answer most or all of these six questions: Who? What? When? Where? Why? How? So, begin by taking the material you have assembled for your story and try to answer them. Some may not apply to a particular story. "How," for

example, will not figure in the announcement of a routine meeting. "Why," too, often will not apply. So ignore them.

But be sure that you have all the information you need to answer all the questions that do apply to the particular event. Sort it out; study it carefully; figure out what is most important—and what is just supporting detail.

3. Now you are ready to write your "lead," which is the opening paragraph—most often just a one-sentence paragraph.

Once upon a time it was newspaper practice to include in the lead answers to all six basic story questions, or to as many as belonged in the particular story. Such leads were long and so choked with information that they were hard to read and dull.

Today the straight news lead is a brief presentation of the major facts of a story. You must grab the reader's interest with the strongest points you have to offer. The rest you leave to be developed later in the story.

To make this clearer, let's start by taking a lead for a story with which everyone is familiar—the wedding announcement:

> Miss Frances Bray, daughter of Mr. and Mrs. Robert Bray of 110 Walton Road, became the bride of Randolph Aubrey, son of Mr. and Mrs. William Aubrey of Granada Boulevard, Saturday at St. Luke's Church. The Rev. Lawrence Mivlonson officiated.

Here we have the "who" (the names of the main participants, with addresses), the "what" (a marriage ceremony), the "where" (the church), the "when" (Saturday), and the "how" (the minister). The "why" is unnecessary because it is well understood that the newlyweds are in love and expect to live happily ever after.

41

This is a standard type of lead for wedding stories. It shows how a lead answers the basic news story questions. However, it also points up how trying to pack all the main information into the beginning makes for a long lead. This is unavioidable as a rule with this type of story because the society editor is trying to cover as many weddings as possible in limited space. But it is something to be avoided in other types of stories.

Let's take another example:

> Twenty Fairfield residents were honored for lengthy service to the Boy Scouts at an awards dinner last night in the Fairfield Cultural Center.

Here we have a lead that answers all six basic news story questions. And it does so in less than 25 words.

You may even find circumstances where an effective lead can ignore most of the basic requirements, as in the settlement of a long controversy:

> The Elm Tree Battle is over at last!

A lead such as this would be acceptable when the community has exhibited intense interest in the controversy and is fully aware of what this particular story is all about. No need to clutter up the start of this story.

This is an exception, however, and generally your job will be to construct as short a lead as you possibly can that will contain the major facts you have to present.

Familiarize yourself with the sample releases at the back of this guide. The first two, on pages 125 and 126, are examples of two approaches to the same subject. It is a good idea to study the publications you will be serving with your publicity releases. Make a habit of clipping out examples of stories that interest you and cover events similar to the ones your organization has.

4. Your lead having been written, now go to work on the rest of your story.

The basic thing to keep in mind here is that the editor is always crowded for space and he may have to "cut" or shorten your story. He doesn't have time to condense it by rewriting it and, in fact, if the story is already in type, it is too late to rewrite, anyway. His only alternative, if he is to use the story at all, is to drop off a paragraph or two from the bottom, sometimes even more.

Therefore, a good news story should be so constructed that it can be cut progressively upward from the bottom, trimming the extra details but still presenting the main facts in the lead and any other paragraphs that escape the blue pencil.

Newspapermen have different names for this construction. Some call it the pyramid style, others, the inverted pyramid. Regardless, this is the way they write and the way you should write.

Returning to our earlier example of the scouting awards dinner, the lead could be followed in successive paragraphs by (a) the most significant award—who won it and why; (b) the next highest awards—what they were for and a list of who received them; (c) those honored in the next category; (d) those honored in successively lesser categories; (e) remarks by the master of ceremonies in bestowing the honors; (f) history about the awards ceremony; and (g) additional detail about the service of any of the top winners.

A story constructed in this fashion could have sections (g), (f) and (e) cut off if the editor had a space problem, and it would still communicate the essential news and get in all the important names.

5. In your writing, use short words; use concrete nouns; use active verbs. Strive for clear, forceful English. The Bible packs a lot of meaning into two words when it says: "Jesus wept." Two words. Compare them with, "Jesus broke out into tears," or, "Jesus began sobbing."

6. Avoid adjectives and adverbs. Don't write that a ceremony was "colorful" or an event "exciting." If you describe it correctly, anyone will know that it was colorful or exciting without having to take your word for it.

7. Don't editorialize. Stick to the facts and use comments only if you can quote someone—and only then if the comments are significant.

8. Shun slang, jargon, clichés and the "fashion" words that are in today, on everyone's lips, but forgotten tomorrow. Steer clear of the coined and tortured words that especially come out of Washington. And don't take the sports pages (or the sports announcers) as your model.

9. A straight line is the shortest distance between two points, but you get tired of all single lines in architecture. Likewise, if every lead you write is brief and straightforward like a sentence in a first-grade primer, you and your readers will suffer from ennui. But if you use concrete nouns and active verbs . . . if you search your story material carefully for a picturesque fact . . . if you are imaginative but careful . . . you can be interesting while still being brief and direct.

10. Don't bother to attribute a routine announcement to anyone in your organization. It adds nothing except needless words to write, "Mrs. Harrison Dobbins, president of the Garden Club, announced that next month's regular meeting June 14 will be devoted to cleaning up the local

environment." But it does add authority to name a source when you have important news and when you can quote that authority in your story on the significance of the announcement.

11. Be specific about when an event occurred, or will occur. If you write "next month," name the month in parentheses so the editor will make no mistake about when you mean. If you write "today," or "Saturday," or "next Saturday," put the correct dates within parentheses. They will be deleted when the copy is edited for publication.

12. Keep your story as short as possible, but when you have finished the first draft, review it carefully with pencil in hand. Cross out superfluous words—pet adjectives that may have crept in. See if you can tighten up your prose by rephrasing clauses. And finally recheck every point for accuracy—names, addresses, titles, dates, figures, everything. When you are satisfied, turn to the section on Copy Preparation for the next step—typing your story for delivery to the publications.

Features

In writing a feature, you are bound by no rules. So long as what you produce is interesting, you can write your own ticket.

Thus, the point of this section is not to tell you how to write a feature—for there is no set pattern and the material itself will dictate what you can do—but to urge you to look beyond your news assignment for feature opportunities. Be inquisitive; find out what your people are doing in their spare time; ask questions; keep your ears open; and familiarize yourself with the archives, if you are lucky enough to have them.

As pointed out in Chapter III, a feature, like a news story, must be interesting. But unlike a news story, it does not have the urgency of a today or yesterday or tomorrow angle. The point of interest does not come from its spot news value—but from some other element.

As the public relations chairman for the local Garden Club, you discover that the top-prize winner at your flower show suffers from rose fever and other flower-pollen allergies. The winning of the prize was a news story when it happened. A human interest story on why and how the winner persevered in flower growing in the face of the allergy handicap would make an interesting follow up.

Thus, the surprise twist is one of the elements you should look for in any situation. Similarly, the top-prize winner at your annual Bake Fair may be a gourmet cook who used to "hate" cooking. What changed her outlook? Dig into her history—and you may find a fascinating feature.

Unusual hobbies are good feature material and they could be good publicity for your organization if they reflect subjects in which your organization is interested. Thus, if your organization is an historical society and you have a member who has a fabulous collection in line with the society's interests, a worthwhile feature could be developed.

Anniversaries are an excellent source of features both on institutions and people. The archives can be searched for interesting institutional history for features timed for a significant anniversary—such as the 50th, the 75th, the 100th. People can be interviewed for their recollections, which could be part of an institutional feature, or features on their personal anniversaries.

If you get a feature idea, a good place to start is to review it with your contact on one of your publication outlets. The publication may want to assign a feature writer of its own to develop the story—or you may get the go-ahead yourself.

A feature should be developed exclusively for one publication. Pick out a newspaper that uses a lot of features, or select a magazine. In fact, a feature may be your only opportunity of getting visibility in certain magazines. If you choose to approach a magazine, do so with an outline of what you have to offer, for the magazine may want to develop the story itself.

Fact Sheets

A fact sheet is an outline designed to give news or background information in highlight form.

It is a valuable communications tool for providing information for a newsman who expects to write his own story, for an editorial writer's background, for a speaker, or for a visitor.

Fact sheets can be sent out in advance of an event to provide information for a pre-event story. They can be handed out to newsmen attending the event to provide them with basic facts and background. They can be kept on hand at headquarters not only for visitors and prospective members, but for sending out to anyone asking for information.

A fact sheet should contain the same who, what, when, where, why and how information as a news release—but in itemized, easily grasped form. When appropriate, supplementary material, such as photographs, may be attached.

To write a fact sheet, do exactly as you do in the beginning for a news story—gather all possible information on the subject. Then break it up into its who, what, when, where, why and how components—beginning with the one that is the most important. You can even head each section with one of these questions. (See sample fact sheets on pages 156 and 158.)

If the fact sheet deals with a building project, tell what it is for, its size, cost, special features, construction timetable, architects and contractors. If it deals with an anniversary, put in dates, significant organization accomplishments through the years and celebration plans. If it deals with a special club project, such as a public seminar, put in the purpose; the subject; the time, date and place; and the speakers.

LAYMAN'S PUBLICITY GUIDE

Radio and Television

While newspapers are the principal channels for community publicity, don't overlook radio and television in your publicity work. Radio and television stations provide millions of dollars worth of free public service time each year for worthwhile community projects. There is one basic requirement—public service announcements *must* be on behalf of *nonprofit* organizations.

If you are serving a nonprofit group, you will find that some of what you prepare for publications will be acceptable to the broadcast media—such as news releases for newscasts and fact sheets for background information—but that in the main you are entering a whole new world.

Because time and available facilities vary widely from station to station, your first step should be to listen to or to watch every one of them serving your area. Become thoroughly familiar with their programs—what they're like and how they're handled.

Then, when you have a project of widespread interest you consider worth discussing, call and make an appointment with the news director of each station, if yours is a news project. You will want to see the program director, if it is a program idea, or, in the case of some of the larger stations, the director of public services or director of community services. Find out how what you have to offer fits in with what each station offers in its air time, and what you must do to provide the material.

You will find a wide variety of opportunities in public service programming for it includes the following:

Specials. Among specials are interviews (live or recorded), group discussions, panel discussions, demonstrations, etc. A special may be a single presentation, or it may be a part of a running series.

Segments. These are similar to specials, but are shorter

presentations used as "participating" features of other programs.

Spots. Live or recorded, these are brief announcements made at various times during a broadcast day. An example would be spots aired to call attention to the current celebration of a special week, such as Girl Scout Week. (See sample releases on pages 129 and 130.)

Personality Spots. These are announcements by on-the-air personalities, such as disc jockeys, directors of farm programs, or directors of women's features, fitting in with their subjects.

News Items. These are news stories included in regular local newscasts, or announcements of scheduled events in calendar-type news presentations.

Editorials. Like newspapers, stations may present their own viewpoints on community activities. Your approach should be the same as outlined in this manual for working with newspaper editorial writers.

Your initial interest usually should be to determine how a station prefers to receive news. It may be that the staff will take your regular news releases, just as you write them for publications, and handle the rewriting itself.

If the preference is for a release in radio news script form, you still will cover the same elements of who, what, when, where, why and how. (See sample release on page 128.) Sentences should be short and construction, simple. Moreover, you should use descriptive words that will help the listener form a picture in his own mind of what you are trying to portray. Be informal. Use "let's" instead of "let us," for example.

Time spot announcements, as detailed in section on "Copy Preparation," striving always for the greatest brevity consistent with clarity and completeness. (See sample release on page 128.)

For television, check with the program or news director regarding slides, films, photographs, products or other visuals which will help demonstrate your message. Slides are preferred to photographs. When photographs are used, matte or dull-surfaced prints should be provided because glossy prints reflect studio lights.

As radio and television needs are specialized, rely on your contacts at the stations for guidance. Also, ask one of the stations for a copy of *If You Want Air Time,* a booklet prepared by the National Association of Broadcasters, with Do and Don't advice and six samples of scripts. Or write direct to NAB at 1771 N Street, N.W., Washington, D.C. 20036.

Copy Preparation

Having drafted your release, you should put it in a form that is acceptable by the publications on your list. If radio and television stations also are among your outlets, they will require a different form of presentation of your information. Refer to the sample releases at the back of this guide as you go through the following instructions.

The News Release

1. Stories must be typed. Use plain paper of standard 8½" x 11" business size. White paper is preferred, but if you want to establish an identity for your organization with a colored stock, use a light yellow or only the palest of pastels. (A pale green would be distinctive for garden club releases, for example.) Use a good quality paper, never the onion-skin second sheets used in business for file copies. Releases should be double-spaced, except for those publications that may tell you they prefer triple spacing.

2. Every publication on your list should receive an original copy. Carbon copies not only are harder to read, particularly if there are a number in a set, but the words will

smudge as the editor does his editing. For your own files, however, a carbon copy should be satisfactory.

3. Margins should be ample. If you have a typewriter with elite type, simply set the margins for body copy at 15 and 85. If your typewriter has larger type, set the margins so that you have about an inch and one-fourth margin at the right and left of your body copy.

4. Next, in the upper right-hand corner, starting at space 65 if you have elite type, type the word FROM: in capital letters and the name of your organization.

On successive lines, flush left under the organization, type your name, address and telephone number, and two lines below that the date. If the name of your organization is a long one, start your FROM line before space 65 or put the name of your organization on two lines, like this:

FROM: FAIRFIELD EDUCATION
COUNCIL
Mrs. Frank Newston
1484 Fifth Avenue
Fairfield, Ct. 06430
(203) 322-0585

April 8, 1976

5. If you are sending your release to a particular department or editor, type an attention line in capitals on the same line as your telephone number beginning at space 15 on the left, as: ATTENTION: SCHOOL PAGE EDITOR. Or, ATTEN-TION: WOMEN'S EDITOR. Or, ATTENTION: (insert editor's name). Underline.

6. Two lines below that, on the same line as the date, also in capital letters and underlined, type release instructions. Normally this line will read:

FOR IMMEDIATE RELEASE.   However, there may be occasions when a specific time is important, such as the actual delivery of a speech or an announcement at a public assembly, or a particular day. If you must specify a time, start one line higher than <u>FOR IMMEDIATE RELEASE,</u> and do it this way:

<u>FOR RELEASE AT 4 P.M., EDT</u>
<u>TUESDAY, APRIL 8</u>

7. To summarize the foregoing, your release now will look like this:

FROM: FAIRFIELD EDUCATION
       COUNCIL
Mrs. Frank Newston
1484 Fifth Avenue
Fairfield, Ct. 06430
(203) 322-0585

<u>FOR IMMEDIATE RELEASE</u>   April 8, 1976

<u>ATTENTION: SCHOOL PAGE EDITOR</u>

8. Next, leave a blank space of about six lines in which the editor can write his headline. Once you have developed experience in preparing releases, you may want to try your hand at writing headlines yourself. A good way to start is to study your outlets to see the kinds of headlines they use and to follow them as models. A headline has to tell a story but it also has to fit—that is, the number of characters in a head must fit the space available. The function of a headline on your release should be the same as the function of a headline in a newspaper—to attract attention and to develop a reader's interest. A good headline may "sell" an editor on your release.

9. Now, type your story. The first sentence of each paragraph

is indented five spaces. The interval between paragraphs is a double space; only rarely a triple space.

If your outlets include out-of-town publications some distance away, and especially in another state, your story should begin with a dateline. Indent five spaces and write the name of your city in capitals and the abbreviation for your state in capital and lower case letters. If the date is important, as it might be in a release on an important speech, that goes next. Thus: FAIRFIELD, Ct., April 8 --.

In most cases, however, your work will be with local media and there will be no need for a dateline. Instead, you will launch directly into your release.

If there are names or titles or any other information in a release that is unusual, it is wise to put the word "correct," within parentheses, after the unusual. Thus, if a person's name is Meginnis, write (correct) after it so the editor won't assume you meant McGinnis and so change it.

10. If your release can be accommodated on one page of paper, signify that it is complete by typing in three number symbols (# # #) two lines below the last line of text and centered under it.

11. If your release requires more than one page, end the first page with the word "more" typed within parentheses two lines below the last line of text and at the right, beginning at space 85 if you have elite type. Thus: (more).

12. When a release requires more than one page, never divide a word between pages. As you see you are nearing the end of the first page in your typing, try to end your copy with a complete paragraph or at least with a complete sentence. If that means leaving an extra amount of white space at the bottom of that page, that's all right.

13. Begin the second page, and any succeeding pages, with

its number and a few words in parentheses to identify the story in the upper left-hand corner, as: (page 2—Acme Award). If any of your outlets prefer that you also put in the name of your organization, do so. Continue your release three spaces below. And, as previously noted, on whatever page you complete it, use the three number symbols (# # #) to signify completion.

14. If your release is accompanied by a photograph, a brochure or any other illustrative or explanatory material, this should be noted at the bottom of the last page of your release. After the number symbols (# # #), two lines lower and over to the left-hand margin, write: Accompanying material: and under that list what you are sending.

15. Check your typed releases carefully for accuracy. Names are particularly important, as are dates. Check addresses. Check for typing errors. Then, do what you have to do to make delivery to meet each publication's deadline.

16. In the event that you serve so many outlets with your releases that typing an original copy for each would be a difficult task, copies that have been mimeographed or otherwise duplicated are acceptable. However, these do not make as good an impression upon an editor as individually typed releases.

Picture Captions

Pictures and other illustrations that accompany releases must carry captions that identify the subjects pictured. This enables the editor to associate them with the proper releases and their sources.

1. To type a caption, use the same kind of paper as you do for releases, but start your typing about three inches down from the top. This provides space for pasting the caption onto the photograph.

2. Use all the information you typed at the head of the first page of your release—the source information and date at the upper right-hand, and release instructions at the left. Above the latter, however, insert the words: <u>Photo to accompany:</u> and under that line identify your release either with its headline, if you wrote a headline, or its subject, such as Acme Award.

3. Beginning two spaces under the release instructions, type the text of your caption. If you are identifying a group of people, specify the order, in parentheses, in which you are describing them, as: (Seated, left to right), (Second row, left to right), (Standing, left to right), etc. Normally, identification is from left to right, but a common exception is where the receiver of an award is pictured standing right. Right and left identification is not necessary where names alone suffice, such as when a high school girl receiving an award is the only girl in the photograph. Close your caption the same way as your release by typing the end symbols (# # #) two spaces below the last line.

4. Using the pasting strip you left at the top of the caption, take rubber cement, paste or clear adhesive tape to fasten it to the back of the picture at its bottom. Then, fold the caption up over the face of the picture. Since your caption will be brief, trim off the blank paper. Thus, when the editor looks at the picture, he unfolds the caption and he has in front of him the photograph and at its bottom, the description.

5. Do *not* use paper clips, as they will leave indentations that may spoil a photograph for reproduction, and do *not* write on the back of a photograph, as the pressure of pen or pencil can damage the surface of a print.

6. If your photograph is too small for the width of your caption paper, mount it on a piece of cardboard.

7. In delivering photographs, protect them with cardboard.

Features

1. In typing a feature story, start the same way as for a news release, with the source information in the upper right-hand corner.

2. When a feature story is prepared for only one publication, at the left, where you wrote FOR IMMEDIATE RELEASE in a news release, you should write:

   EXCLUSIVE TO (NAME OF PUBLICATION). Like the news release, it can carry the attention slug line if you want to direct it to a particular editor or department.

3. Except for the foregoing, the typing of a feature follows the same pattern as the news release—with one exception. While a news release will run one or two pages, a feature may be lengthy. To break up the solid text, you should consider two devices—section heads and subheads.

When an article has natural sections, each section should be introduced with a section head. Section heads should be typed in upper and lower case letters, flush left with the body text, and should be underlined. If you were to prepare an historical feature about your organization, for example, successive section heads might be: The First Century, Today's New Look, and Planning for the Future.

You will see subheads used in many newspapers to break up long columns of text and you can follow their example—a few appropriate words inserted to introduce the immediately fol- lowing text. A subhead should be typed in the center of a page, in upper and lower case, and it should be underlined. It is double-spaced from the preceding paragraph and from the following paragraph. By choosing your words carefully, you can use subheads to heighten interest in your subject. Be careful, however, not to put them in where they intrude on a running topic.

The Fact Sheet

Because a fact sheet presents information in highlight form, the layout is left to the discretion of the writer. Except for that, typing up a fact sheet follows much the same pattern as the news release.

1. The fact sheet is typed on standard 8½" by 11" paper, with the same source information in the upper right-hand corner as a news release.

2. If it is being sent out as an accompaniment to a news release, it should have the same attention line, exclusivity and release line slugs. If it is being sent out independently, only those slug lines that are appropriate need be used.

3. While it is not necessary for you to write a headline for a news release, you must title a fact sheet. You can do so in any way you want—in the center of the page or at the left. You can use a single line typed all in capital letters and underlined, as: FACT SHEET ON (SUBJECT). Or, depending on how long your subject is, you can break up the title into two or more lines, as:

FACT SHEET ON . . .

(SUBJECT)

4. As to the body of the fact sheet, you can use any style you choose. If you choose the Who? What? When? Where? Why? How? approach, you can head each section with one of these words. You can use single spacing where you want, double spacing where you want, triple spacing or more where you want. You should, however, observe the conventional margins.

5. If the fact sheet runs longer than one page, "(more)" is not typed at the bottom of each page before the last. Second and succeeding pages are numbered, as releases are, with a word or so of identification.

LAYMAN'S PUBLICITY GUIDE

Radio

1. Typewrite all copy triple space on the same 8½" by 11" paper that you use for your press releases, unless your radio station contacts say they will accept double-spaced copy.

2. Put the name of your organization, your own name, address and telephone number, and the date in the upper right-hand corner, as you do on press releases.

3. If there are instructions for release time and date, type them on the left as you do on press releases. Otherwise: <u>FOR BROADCAST AT WILL</u>.

4. If you are providing a news release for a radio news program that duplicates the news release you have written for publications, leaving it to the radio station staff to rewrite, simply repeat your press release but with one new ingredient. Proper names, foreign words and scientific and other terms whose pronunciation might be unfamiliar to the commentator should be given phonetically immediately after their first appearance in the release. Syllables are separated by hyphens, and accented syllables are typed in capital letters, as: Paul Liebel (lee-BELL) of Leicester (LES-ter) County. Never divide a word between lines.

5. If you are providing a spot announcement or other special script, type at the left, under any release instructions, the word "Time:" and the number of seconds the script requires for reading, and under that the word "Words:" and the number of words in the script. Thus: Time: 10 seconds and Words: 25. As a rule of thumb, time spot announcements to run 10 seconds (25 words), 20 seconds (50 words) or 60 seconds (150 words).

6. Check your station contacts on how many copies they want. Usually several copies of all material are needed, and it is expected that all will be legible.

7. If you have arranged an interview, provide a biographical sketch of the person to be interviewed, along with a summary of six or eight points to be covered in the interview.

Television

1. A news release for television that you expect the television station news department to rewrite may be the same as a news release for radio.

2. A release prepared for television use, however, is a different matter. It should show all the information you provide on a radio release—the source information, date, release time and date, time for presentation and the number of words—but here is what is different:

The body of a television release follows an established two-column format. Assuming that you are using a typewriter with elite type (though pica type is preferred for radio and television scripts), start at space 25 and head one column with the word VIDEO—all capital letters and underlined. Then, at space 60, head the second column AUDIO.

In the VIDEO column you will list in their proper places in relation to the AUDIO text the slides, photographs, film or other visual aids to be used for illustration as the copy is read. Number each item and type the information in capital letters, single spacing the copy that runs longer than one line in this narrow column.

In the AUDIO column, beginning at space 60, the text to be read by the announcer or commentator is written. Each item begins with the same number and on the same line as the numbered items in the VIDEO column. Type this information in capital and lower case letters, triple spacing unless your television station contact tells you double spacing will be acceptable.

In timing your copy for the time and word information at the beginning of the release, do so at a slightly slower pace than for radio. Standard announcements for television run 10 seconds (about 20 words—as compared to 25 words on radio); 20 seconds (40 words); and 60 seconds (125 words).

3. One slide or photograph should be provided for each 10-second spot; two for a 20-second spot; and so on up to six for a 60-second spot. Slides usually are preferred to photographs. When the latter are provided, they should be matte or dull-surfaced prints. The glossy prints that publications prefer reflect studio lights when used on television. If you have film available, discuss the station's requirements with the program director.

4. As in radio releases, never divide a word between lines and any word that may be difficult to pronounce should be given the phonetic spelling in parentheses directly after the word.

5. If a television release is more than a spot announcement or brief news release, give it a cover page. Give the source information and release information as you would on any release, but type in capital letters about the center of the page the title of the script and even a subtitle if it will help "sell" the subject. Then, list on the cover page the slides, photographs and other visual material included with the release, as well as the props that must be obtained by the television station. Look to your television station contacts for help. A television script is a specialized undertaking and you should seek the guidance your contacts will give you provided you have the kind of basic material that will make a good television presentation.

V   WHAT ABOUT
PHOTOGRAPHS?

Photographs have never been as important in publicity as they are today because the media demand has never been so great. Wanted are news pictures that are timely . . . dramatic; feature pictures with human interest; pictures that tell a story all by themselves . . . or that enhance the written story.

Should you be concerned with them in your publicity work? A thousand times, yes!

And for these main reasons:

1. Photographs communicate even as words communicate, though with the special advantages of being a quick attraction to the reader's eye and a quick story teller. To go back to the roots of the word "photograph"— *phos-phot*, light, and *graph*, write. Hence, you write with light. In short, another communications tool and, wisely used, a very effective one.

2. Photographs can deliver a message not only to those who don't have the time (or won't take the time) to read, but also to those who may not be able to read or who read poorly.

3. Thanks to television and the creative use of photographs in all types of publications, the public is more picture-conscious than ever before.

4. There has been a tremendous change in the method of printing used by the publications with which you will be

dealing—especially the weekly and small daily newspapers, and regional magazines. Without getting into technical details, the traditional letterpress method has been giving way to offset lithography. This makes it considerably cheaper than before to prepare photographs for publication. Not only does the publisher save money—he gets remarkably improved reproduction quality.

5. Striking advances have been made in photographic equipment. Moderately priced cameras are available that are small, light in weight and easy to handle. Lenses are fast, enabling satisfactory results under variable conditions. Electric eyes read the light and set exposure automatically. Flash equipment is compact and easy to use when the available light is too weak. In short, you don't have to be a prince (or princess) to afford one of these modern marvels—and you don't have to be a professional to operate one. Films are faster, too, making it possible to get satisfactory results under previously impossible conditions. Speedy development and printing are available in many communities.

6. Good photographs still are in short supply. Look at your local newspapers and see for yourself the quality of the content. If the pictures you see are dull and unimaginative, take them as a signal. Seize on what you see as an opportunity to do better—and your publicity results will reward you.

Types of Photographs

There are three main kinds of photographs that deserve your consideration, depending on the depth of your publicity program, the editorial demand and the size of your budget.

(This is one area of your work where having a budget is critical. Photography is an out-of-pocket expense. However little you try to get by with and regardless of who does the work except, of course, in the very rare instances where a newspaper sends a staff photographer. Budgeting will be discussed in a later section.)

In order of importance, here are the three types:

1. *News* pictures—to go along with the stories you write about current events in your organization.

2. *Feature* pictures—to accompany the written features you may develop, or that tell a story all by themselves—either alone or as a group making up a picture story.

3. *Record* pictures—to supplement the news and feature photographs in building up the archives of your organization, for bulletin board or lobby displays, to illustrate the annual report, or for projection at special meetings or on special occasions, such as an open house.

News pictures. Because the bulk of your effort—perhaps even your whole effort—will be devoted to communicating news about your organization, *news* pictures will be your main photographic concern.

When new officers are elected, your announcement release should be accompanied by a photograph of the president or a shot of the whole group, if it is relatively small.

If you have a program featuring a prominent speaker, a photograph could be a valuable part of your advance publicity, and photographic coverage at the actual event should be a part of your planning.

If your organization undertakes a new building program, the photographic possibilities are endless as the project advances. With the initial announcement, a picture of the building committee looking at a blueprint or a scale model would be acceptable, and throughout the project there will be major milestones worth recording—including breaking ground; laying the cornerstone; "topping-out" ceremony; dedication; etc.

Earlier in this guide, in the preliminary steps for getting started on the handling of publicity, a study of the media outlets and chats with editors on what they wanted were recommended . . . for photographs as well as written information.

With that spadework accomplished, and full knowledge of your organization's program of activities and events, picking out the publicity worth illustrating should be relatively easy. As a rule, you'll want to show a key person or a key group. Any major announcement will attract more attention if it is accompanied by an appropriate photograph.

Feature pictures.   Earlier, in Chapter III, a written feature was described as "a story that must be interesting—but unlike a news story it does not have the urgency of a today or yesterday or tomorrow angle." It may be appealing because of human interest. Or, a familiar example is an anniversary feature.

For an anniversary feature, it is obvious that there should be good illustrations—both the kind you will find in the archives and present-day photographs that will bring the chronicle up to date. If there are no archives, see what you can dig out from your library, the historical society, and the albums of long-time members.

However, feature pictures are not limited to companion material for written features; they have an important role of their own. They can tell some kinds of stories all by themselves.

You see feature pictures in your newspapers all the time. A familiar variety is the seasonal picture. In the spring, the first robin, or the photograph an alert cameraman snapped when a naked youngster wandered out of the house into the yard, or young lovers sitting on a bench in the park. Without words, these pictures say one thing: "Spring is here!"

WHAT ABOUT PHOTOGRAPHS?

With a little thought, seasonal picture ideas worth publishing will occur to you. The publicist for a nature center and zoo, for example, has a *news* picture when one of the animals has a bumper litter. But lambs gamboling in the pasture on the first day of spring would create opportunity for a *feature* picture.

But you needn't stop with the seasonal. No matter what your responsibility is—a garden club, a church circle, an international friendship group, or whatever—there are feature photographs that can be taken, and will be used by editors. Study the pictures in the newspapers you read, and in magazines. Go to the library and leaf through publications you may not otherwise see.

Look hard at everything and everyone in your organization for feature possibilities and, if you have to, exert influence to get photogenic projects developed. You'll find generating feature photographs highly rewarding, for not only will you get good visibility for your organization you cannot get with words, but you will have a lot of fun besides.

A word of warning: Any feature picture should be given on an exclusive basis to one publication. In news pictures, prints of one photograph often can be offered to a number of publications without offense. Nevertheless, you'll improve the likelihood of acceptance if you have enough different shots to offer each news photograph also on an exclusive basis.

Besides the feature picture that tells a story all by itself, there are picture stories composed of a group of photographs. Because these take a lot of space, they must have broad general interest. Therefore, when you have an idea for what strikes you as a good picture story, take it to one of your editor friends and have a discussion. Only with an editorial go-ahead is it worth pursuing. But with an editorial go-ahead you will have made a dramatic placement.

Record pictures.   This is a neglected area or one which you may say belongs to your historian, if your organization has one. A

65

historian is responsible for the archives, of course, but record pictures have other uses too which are in the domain of publicity. For example, if you stage an open house, a good display of photographs in the lobby or on a bulletin board or on a group of easels could go a long way toward informing your visitors of the range of your activities.

Similarly, for a visual report on the past year at your annual meeting or for a special presentation to prospective members in a membership drive, pictures that would not qualify for newspaper use nevertheless could have in-house importance and value.

In taking news or feature pictures for publication, black-and-white photographs are what you will be providing. But in taking record pictures don't overlook color photography for slide shows.

Who's the Photographer?

A photographic assignment may be carried out by any of the following:

1. Staff photographers of publications.

2. Professional photographers hired by you.

3. Amateur photographers, perhaps members of your organization.

4. Yourself.

Staff photographers. Among the questions when you first talk with editors about your publicity role should be whether a publication has a staff photographer and, if so, what kinds of assignments are usually covered. You probably will find that many of your publicity outlets have no photographer at all, and that those who do give precedence in their coverage to spot news events, such as fires and automobile accidents, which can occur at any time, and ceremonies and functions close at home of broad public interest.

WHAT ABOUT PHOTOGRAPHS?

When you have a top-drawer event of your own coming up, it is a good idea to discuss it in advance with your editorial contacts. You should outline the picture possibilities and make a point of inviting them to send their staff photographers.

Don't be disappointed if your invitation is refused. You should then determine what kinds of photographs might be considered, to guide you in taking them or having them taken. Where an event lends itself to a preliminary shooting session, you'll help to ensure coverage by offering to set up such a session at a photographer's convenience.

If your invitation to cover the actual event is accepted, don't be disappointed if the photographer fails to show up. Sudden news emergencies will take precedence.

Thus, to be sure of obtaining satisfactory photographic coverage, your only alternative is to arrange to have it done. Otherwise, you'll have to do it yourself.

Professional photographers. If you don't know a good professional, perhaps your editorial contacts can guide you to one with whose work they are familiar. If an assignment is on a weekend or after regular hours at night, a newspaper photographer may be available as a free lance. Or check with camera stores.

The advantages of professionals are that they have the proper equipment and the experience. They not only are qualified to take good pictures, but usually have the facilities for processing the film and prints expeditiously to meet quick deadlines. And they're available when you want them.

Such services, of course, cost money. In preparing to set up a budget, you should find out what the costs are by contacting a number of photographers. Some charge by the hour, or the half day, or full day, undertaking to provide a certain number of shots in the time period. There are extra charges for extra prints. All this information should be gathered in advance.

LAYMAN'S PUBLICITY GUIDE

Whenever you hire a professional, be specific on what the assignment is and have a specific understanding of what you are going to get and what it will cost. If, for example, you merely want a couple of shots of a speaker delivering a speech, or of your newly elected president or group of new officers, or of an award ceremony, ask what the minimum fee will be and how many different shots are allowed by the fee. If you are staging a seminar with a panel of speakers, realize that tying up a photographer for considerable time just to get action pictures of each speaker may cost more than you can afford. A group picture, posed in advance of the opening of the program, may very well serve your purposes. Explore the possibilities in advance with the photographer. Make sure that you have everything set up for the photographer so the assignment can be accomplished in minimum time. You'll save money.

Amateur photographers. In your organization there may be qualified amateurs willing, as members doing their part for the common cause, to take the photographs you need. Or a member may have a youngster who is a camera buff who can handle your assignments. Failing those, check your local camera club for volunteers.

The cost for film and processing services is minimal. But you should be assured, particularly for news pictures, that quick processing is possible so that you can meet publication deadlines.

Yourself. Assuming you have the equipment, the experience and the desire, you may well double as the publicity writer and the photographer. No one has a greater interest and no one has a better understanding of what you are trying to accomplish.

Whether someone else takes the pictures, you are the one who must map out what is to be taken. You are the one who decides what is wanted and who must superintend, whether the photographer is sent by a publication, is a professional hired by you, or an amateur, or even yourself telling yourself what to do. As the director anyway, using the camera is little extra effort. Moreover, you are attending an event because you have to be there to write about it, so you are available.

This may be the only answer to your problem of photography—but don't overlook this before you decide: Tying yourself up with picture-taking can interfere with your coverage of a story. If you're taking notes while a speech is being delivered, you're not able to take an action photograph of the speaker. Wearing two hats can pose difficulties.

Some assignments, of course, will lend themselves to your serving in a dual role. Covering an open house, for example, calls for circulating around for story purposes as well as photographs. Combining the roles should not be difficult.

Your decision may be to do as much photography as you can without interfering with your writing assignment, and arranging for others to take the pictures when you cannot do so. That way you can get it all done for the least amount of money.

The Budget

If you inherited a budget when you assumed your publicity responsibility, you know what you can spend. Whether it is enough to accomplish what you may want to do is another matter.

So, budget or no budget, you should put together all the information you can on the costs of photography. Contact a number of professionals and get their charges for various types of assignments. Find out what film and processing will cost if you or some other amateur takes the pictures.

Then sit down with the activities and events on your organization's program and map out the *news* picture possibilities. Figure out your needs and probable time for each assignment, and cost these assignments out to get the over-all total for a year.

Next, study the *feature* picture possibilities. These will lend themselves to amateur photography. And don't forget that if you interest a newspaper in a picture story, it undoubtedly would prefer to send a staff photographer. Costs in this category could be minimal.

Finally, address yourself to what uses there may be for *record* pictures. Keep in mind here that you may be selling some new ideas to the leaders in your organization, and progress may be slow. However, photograhy in this category lends itself to amateurs, so film and processing costs are all you have to estimate. In addition, if there will be use for slides for special presentations, take into account the costs of color film and processing.

Once you have developed a tentative budget, you must present it for approval. If it's cut down, you will have to scale down your photographic expenses accordingly. Or, even better, arrange for amateur photography.

Delivering the Product

In your discussions with editorial contacts, the questions you need answered include deadlines for photographs, to whom they should be delivered, and any specifications on size and finish.

Publications usually prefer 8 x 10 prints, glossy finish, good contrast. But you may find that smaller prints will be accepted. Horizontal or vertical formats usually are acceptable.

Each photograph should have an appropriate caption identifying individuals from left to right and telling the what, when and where of the story. Captions should be typed and pasted or taped on the bottom edge of a picture. Captions should contain also your name, address and telephone number.

When you send a photograph, always protect it with cardboard. Never send it unprotected in an envelope—and *never* fold it. And never use paper clips; they leave crease marks that mar the photograph. And finally, never write on the back of a photograph with a pen or hard pencil. If you must write on the back, use a very soft pencil with a very soft touch. Better still, type up a slip of paper and paste it on the back of the photo.

If possible, send together both the story and the photograph it illustrates. If they are delivered separately, include a carbon copy of the story with the picture, or a note, so the editor can readily put the two together.

It is not wise to ask for the return of a photograph. Most of the time, requests for return are an annoyance. If returned, the photographs inevitably will be defaced, having been marked up for publication. In connection with a studio photograph of, say, your new president, which you must use because it is all that is available, you have two courses. If time permits, have a photo service copy the picture and provide you with prints. If it doesn't, level with your editor friends, ask them to take all possible care of the picture, and request its return.

Proper Planning

Good pictures don't just happen.

Some outstanding pictures you have seen resulted from a little luck. Someone with a camera happened to be in the right spot at the right time and pressed the right button. Such photographs are few and far between.

Most of the good pictures you see were not shot from the hip. They were the product of some planning, some advance thinking about the subject and the situation, and some idea of what to do and when to do it.

To take a candid shot, for example, you could just blaze away—and then sift the results to see what is good. Or you could be all set up—right focus, right shutter setting, right aperture—

and, knowing a bit about the subject and what you wanted to take, wait patiently for the right moment to go into action.

Whether you hire a professional—or go with an amateur—or take the pictures yourself, you are the one who must do the planning . . . and the thinking . . . and the superintending. Don't assume that because you have a professional taking pictures, you will have spectacular photographs. The quality will be good, but unless there is a definite story idea the result can be flat and pedestrian—a competent record shot and nothing more.

All this means that if you have no photographic background, you ought to start getting one. Go to a camera store and pick up some basic instruction books. Go to the library and study the photo magazines. And talk to your editorial contacts and to your friends who are camera buffs. Use a camera yourself and do some experimenting.

This is not intended to be a photographic handbook, but here are a few basic tips:

Don't have a subject stand with both body *and* head facing directly toward the camera. Instead, have the person (or persons) stand at an angle from the camera, with only the head turned to it. You'll get a more relaxed pose and a much more interesting picture.

Have your subjects doing something. To pose them like wooden Indians staring into the camera will assure you of flat, uninteresting pictures. If your building committee is considering a number of designs, have them looking at a model or a plan. Or show them on the site where the building will be erected. Show your new president in a setting appropriate to his or her background, or appropriate to your organization.

Avoid taking large groups. Some authorities suggest three or four persons in a picture are maximum. It often will be difficult to hold to such an arbitrary maximum, but try to hold the number down as much as you can. If you have a 10-person executive committee, there's nothing you can do about it. But if you have a 50-person membership captain group, break them up into their geographic areas or other units.

Watch poses. Individuals, and individuals in groups, should appear as natural as possible. Put them at ease by chatting.

Watch backgrounds. Where you can move your subjects around, do so when you must avoid cluttered, dirty or busy backgrounds. Avoid having a sidewall lighting fixture appearing as though it were coming out of the top of a person's head.

Panel sessions—where a group is sitting at a table and a speaker is at the mike—pose a number of problems. There are different values of light on the subjects and always there is the risk of showing one or another with head turned away, or head looking down at a paper, or body slumped comfortably but not gracefully. To have greater control, try posing the group before or after the actual proceedings.

If you're taking your own pictures, select the right film for the job. If, for example, you are taking pictures inside, and expect to use available light, you need the fastest film you can get. There are many tricks photographers know, so quiz them for help. Tri-X film, for example, has an ASA rating of 400—but you can set your camera for 800 ASA and get good results under poor light conditions. The only thing is you must be sure to tell your film processor so he will develop at 800 ASA.

When you are taking flash pictures, realize that the flash carries only a short distance. You've seen people in a stadium or a theater taking flash pictures at a distance, a wasted effort. Be reasonable; know the limitations of your camera, your film and your flash equipment.

Shooting inside by available light catches the naturalness of a setting and of a group. But it may be risky. So use a flash, but bounce it off the ceiling, if it is low enough, or from the walls, to get a soft and well-rounded effect.

Don't get too arty. The blending of fine tones that gives the exhibition print its great quality is easily lost on the newspaper press; what will attract attention in a salon will be a disappointment in your newspaper.

For the same reason, be careful about studio portraits. If you must use head shots, contrasty prints are much better. And check with your editorial contacts on their preference—light or dark backgrounds.

The goal of your publicity program is to build a good image for your organization. Good photograhps will reflect that image.

VI INVITING THE PRESS

Your understanding with the press should be that it is welcome at all times to cover any meeting, function or event that it may consider promising for a news story or a feature—or even just for its general background on your organization.

But—reinforce the open invitation with specific invitations each time you have a major project of unusual public interest or a popular social event.

The Open Invitation

In your exploratory conversations to establish your contacts with the press, make a point of telling them that they have an open invitation to attend any of your calendared activities. They'll quickly tell you when they may have the time and the interest for personal coverage. As your contacts change, keep telling the new ones that they are welcome.

Besides being invited to attend any function on your program, a reporter should feel free to come in at any mutually convenient time to develop a special feature or to gather public information.

The only time a line is drawn in the open-door policy is when purely internal affairs of an organization are involved. But anything of bona fide public interest should be open to view.

However, with small staffs, many areas to cover, and pressing deadlines, the local press is severely limited in its personal coverage. You may be told that your organization may rarely, if ever, expect a reporter to show up. You shouldn't be surprised and you shouldn't be offended. And you shouldn't be dismayed, for this is exactly why you have the publicity job, in the first place. You are the eyes, and ears, and even the nose of the press people who simply just don't have much time for personal coverage. The opportunity thus is all yours to develop the material that will be interesting enough to command attention.

You could, of course, encounter some surprises. Officially, the press may not have time for the meetings you hold and the events you stage. But what a journalist may do on his own time is up to him. If you are doing publicity for a garden club, for example, one of your press contacts may be a gardening buff. He or she may enjoy what your organization is doing for personal reasons—and you gain the benefit of personal coverage. Or, a contact may already be a member of your organization.

The Special Invitation

Special invitations should be issued to the press whenever you have an event of unusual community importance or when the press may want to develop its own particular approach, such as in an interview with a visiting dignitary. Invitations, accompanied by free tickets, also should be extended for luncheon or dinner meetings, and for dances and balls.

Here is a brief checklist of some of the projects in a community organization that would qualify for special press invitations:

- The kickoff of a new building program or other major physical undertaking.
- The announcement of an important new community service project.
- The dedication and formal opening of new facilities.
- The formal opening of an anniversary celebration.
- The annual banquet (a "courtesy" invitation, if it is a social event; a "working" invitation if a prominent speaker or panel of speakers is on the program).

- A roundtable conference or seminar.
- A special press conference—to interview a distin-
  guished visitor or to announce a major new program.
- An exhibition or show.
- An open house if displays are noteworthy.
- An outstanding acquisition (rare books, antiques,
  etc.)
- A demonstration.

Note that such events as the annual induction of officers or other routine activities do not qualify. Instead, provide coverage of such events with your own releases.

When the Press Arrives

When you invite the press, you should be well prepared to handle your guests. You should greet them on arrival and make them feel at home. Introduce them to your principals; provide guides if the event is an open house, show or exhibition; provide properly briefed officials or other authorities to give authoritative answers; do everything you can to answer their questions and serve their needs.

If the occasion is a banquet with a top-flight speaker, a press table may be in order. You should sit there, too, and offer any assistance that may be required by your press guests. Find out in advance whether the speaker has a prepared text. If he does, get it and make enough copies to distribute to the press corps. If no advance text is available, perhaps the speaker may be willing to give you an abstract of his speech, which you can copy and circulate.

Similarly, prepare in advance written material appropriate for any press visit—historical highlights of your organization, for example, if you are celebrating a significant anniversary, or, in the case of an exhibition or show, a guide listing the exhibits and describing features.

Check in advance also on photographic requirements. If a newspaper wants to send a staff photographer to photograph a speaker, inquire whether there is a preference for a special set-up before the actual speech or a photograph during the delivery. An advance photographic session, where perhaps the speaker is greeted by your president or executive committee, will enable the photographer to get a usable picture with minimum expenditure of time. Similarly, for any type of event, determine photographic requirements and cooperate in providing special shooting sessions if they are requested. If you are expected to provide the photographs, find out what each publication is interested in getting, and brief the photographer you hire accordingly.

If the event has an interest for radio or television stations, establish in advance what special facilities they may require, or what coverage you might provide in the form of tapes, photographs or written releases.

If a reporter accepts your press invitation, but fails to show up, don't be disturbed. A reporter may be called out on an emergency assignment and must break his date with you. If you have a chance to clear with him in advance what he may want in such an eventuality, you'll know what to do for him; otherwise, use your judgment and pick up the kind of story information you think he'll like. And get it to him as fast as you can so he can write his story.

The Interview

Setting up an interview for the press is an excellent way to get good visibility for your organization—if what you have to offer is of sufficient importance or interest to the community to justify a reporter's time.

You may be concerned with one or both of two types of interviews:

- The news interview, designed to develop information on a subject in the news.

- The personality interview, designed to present an individual in the news, or who is interesting even if not in the news, such as one having an unusual hobby.

To explain the difference, let's take possible interviews with two architects:

A *news* interview would be in order with the architect responsible for that unusual new activity center your organization is considering building—giving him a chance to explain in depth his thinking about the over-all concept, how each of the parts contributes to the whole, how the idea originated, why the particular concept best benefits your activity, the flexibility for future expansion, etc. The story is not in the architect himself, but in the explanation of the project he has designed for your community.

On the other hand, suppose your newly elected president happens to be a famous architect better known, perhaps in the outside world where his creations stand, than here at home. A *personality* interview is very much in order—tying together just who this interesting person is, why he is involved in your organization and what he plans to do for you (that is, the community) that is different, meaningful or exciting. The story here is in the individual himself.

You may be rich or poor in interview possibilities, but here are a few prospects:

- The "father" or "mother" behind any new project your organization undertakes which is interesting for what it will do for the community, for its unusualness, for its pioneering, or whatever. This could be the architect responsible for a new design concept, as already mentioned, or the "architect" behind a new service project.

79

- Your new president, or any individual—officer, committee chairman or hired expert—entrusted with a major project of wide importance—in all cases, to introduce a new leader to the community.

- Your veteran president, whose longevity in office itself may be newsworthy, or whose role and recollections may be particularly interesting on an anniversary of your organization. If you are celebrating your 25th, or 50th, or 100th anniversary, for example, an interview with a long-time president or any other individual with an active, long-time role in your organization could help make your history come alive.

- A visiting dignitary. This might be a national or even an international authority who has come to your community for some special reason connected with his work, and is enlisting the help of your organization, or who is just visiting an old friend locally, but may be willing to be interviewed for views on topics of current broad concern.

- Or this visiting dignitary might be a famous actor or actress, an author, or an outstanding athlete. You may have invited such a personality to kick off some great new project you are undertaking—but the press may seize on the opportunity to develop a personality interview.

- The delegate from your organization on his return from an international conference where something of unusual importance occurred.

- Any member with an unusual hobby.

There are all sorts of possibilities—but they must all stand the test of producing information of local importance or of local interest. Keep your eyes open for good prospects, but be honest with yourself if you lack them. Don't try to force a story if there really isn't one, or if it is at best borderline.

Depending upon the nature of your organization, politicians may be prospects or they may be not. Unless there is a real organization benefit, don't compromise. Shun politicians who may be looking only for a convenient platform and who could do your organization's image more harm than good.

Travelers returning from a tour normally are poor copy, for traveling today is a popular pastime and personal experiences, however exciting to the person, seldom impress others. However, you must use your judgment. If your organization is well-known in your community for a project involving a foreign community, anyone visiting that community should have something interesting to report.

In looking over the possibilities, you will note that some prospective interviews deal very clearly with the activities of your organization, such as an anniversary interview with your president. Others may be at best tangential or even irrelevant, such as an interview with a famous athlete just happening to be visiting a member of your organization. Your public relations objective, of course, is to do all you can for your organization. But if, in proposing an irrelevant interview to a reporter, the reporter gets a good story, you still have done a good deed. The press is pleased when you tip it off to anything good—and if you help the press and your organization very little in a particular case, chalk it up to good long-term public relations. It's still worth doing because it helps cultivate a real working relationship.

Having established that you have good potential interview material, how do you go about developing it?

As a rule, only one reporter should be involved. You shouldn't be in a position of playing favorites. If you have multiple outlets, the press conference is indicated. It's discussed in the next section. But if there is only one newspaper that makes a practice of doing good interview stories, you have to be concerned with only that one. Or, if a reporter calls you with his own idea to set up an interview, again, you are concerned with only that one. An interview gives a reporter opportunity to develop his own story—and he does not want to share any special questions or angles he wants to develop with a competitor.

Should you do the interview yourself? Perhaps never; certainly, hardly ever. The purpose of an interview is for a newspaper to explore what it wants to explore, to develop an exclusive story, or to carry out an established format. That is not for an outsider to do who represents and is responsible to the organization sponsoring the interview. Any exceptions would be just that— exceptional. Possible, but not probable.

If you, rather than a reporter, initiate the idea of an interview, first do a thorough job of research so you can outline to a reporter what it is he may expect to get. Then, the idea accepted, work with the person to be interviewed to be sure all pertinent information is gathered. If, for example, your president is to be interviewed on an organization anniversary, prepare an outline and develop a fact sheet of historic dates and milestones in the organization's life. If a reporter initiates the idea of an interview, find out clearly what he wants—and again do the research to prepare the material that will be useful to him.

When the interview takes place, should you be present? Maybe. Maybe not. Often a reporter will resent having any extra persons present. But, to get back to the example of an interview with your president on an anniversary, you could be helpful in bringing out interesting information about your organization if the interview in its normal course should not do so. Or, if some questions were to come up for which there were no ready answers, you could volunteer to get the information. If the interview is with a visiting author, you might not be welcome. However, if an outside photographer is not available and you are good at taking pictures, you may very well provide the needed service.

If you are present, stay in the background unless you have information that is very pertinent. Of course, if your organization is to be the topic of discussion, and somehow the interview starts wandering, it's part of your job to get it back on track. Your assignment always, of course, is to do the best you can for your organization.

One very acceptable reason for your attending an interview could be to take charge of the tape recorder, if there are no objections to being recorded. A tape recording could be a great addition to your archives.

The Press Conference

The press conference is a "mass" interview opportunity for the press.

It may be called to make an important announcement, followed by a question-and-answer session. This is the well-known format of the President's press conferences in the White House or elsewhere.

Or, it may be called to give the local press an equal opportunity to meet a visiting dignitary, where there is no news announcement but merely an exposure opportunity for the press to develop whatever story it can.

A press conference is a ticklish thing to handle—and you shouldn't contemplate one until you are well grounded in your job and sure of your relationships with the press.

And, even then, you shouldn't arrange for one unless you are confident that you have something important and timely—something of genuine worth.

To return to the earlier example of an architect being interviewed for information on that unusual new activity center your organization is planning, a press conference would be in order if you have multiple press outlets to serve. Not only should the architect responsible for the design be put on the platform, but anyone else involved in masterminding the project who could answer questions the public may ask. Put a panel of experts on the platform, if that is what the occasion calls for.

Your role is to set up the press conference when it's important to have one. That means inviting everybody who should be invited. It means assuring that all physical arrangements are properly made—adequate seating, platform, tables, audio equipment, visual aids, etc. Is a blackboard called for? A projector and screen? What kind of projector? It means briefing the speakers on their role—on what to expect from the press. It means preparing any materials that may be appropriate to hand out, such as a fact sheet, architect's renderings, etc. Arrange for any photography that is requested or that you believe may be useful.

At some conferences, it may be best if you are seen and not heard. At others, if the start seems slow, don't hesitate to throw in a question to the platform to get things started, or to keep them moving if the action is slowing down. Also, if no one asks a question that elicits information you want brought out, ask it yourself.

Perhaps you'll be the only one to direct the conference. If so, don't let it wander and don't let it flounder. Direct it to the best of your ability along the lines that will produce the fullest information you had in mind when the press conference idea was conceived. Give the press adequate rein, but guide it gently if it starts straying. And when all the subjects have been well explored, give notice that, "We have time for one or two more questions." When they have been answered, close the conference promptly.

VII   GOING THE EXTRA MILE

You may ask: "Aren't news . . . and features . . . and photographs . . . and interviews more than enough to keep me busy? You mean there's more?"

Yes, there is more to a well-rounded publicity program—more that *can* be done, rather than more that *has* to be done. And if you agree that this more represents worthwhile potential for your organization, but also is more than you can do by yourself, yell for help. If your organization's calendar is a full one, and you have many publicity outlets to serve, you probably need help anyway—either an assistant or even a publicity committee.

What follows consists of two kinds of activities:

1. More publicity opportunities—namely, editorials, letters to the editor and working with clergymen.

2. Calling attention to your publicity results within your own organization—through clipping books, bulletin boards, special displays, etc.

Editorials

Through their editorials newspapers will give special recognition to a local organization for an outstanding achievement or on an important anniversary, or to a project of noteworthy benefit to the community.

But first, if you are new to the world of journalism, you may be confused by the twofold meaning of the word "editorial."

One of its meanings is as a generic word to distinguish the news and feature content of a publication from the advertising content. Thus, a reporter will say that he works "on the editorial side" and he will refer to anyone in the advertising department as being "on the advertising side." Or, a publisher will say that he strives for a 60/40 advertising/editorial ratio in his publication— that is, 60 percent of the total content will comprise paid advertising and the remaining 40 percent, news and features.

Its second meaning is as a word to describe a newspaper or magazine article that gives the opinions of its editors or publishers; of a guest, in the case of a "guest editorial"; or of network or station management, in the case of radio and television.

You'll usually see editorials in the print media on the editorial page, although some publications may start them on the front page, or even run one on the front page on rare occasions to call special attention to it.

It is this second meaning that applies to the suggestion that one of the great opportunities you may have in discharging your publicity responsibility will be to win favorable editorial comment for your organization. This would be in addition to any news announcements you are able to place.

What you are seeking in editorial comment is special recognition, as in the case of an important anniversary; special support, as in the case of the launching of an important community project; or an interpretation of a project that will help the community's understanding and therefore help to win its support. It could be a simple congratulatory message or, at the other extreme, an in-depth exploration of the pros and cons of a major undertaking.

By the definition already given, an editorial gives the opinions of the editors or publishers or management in radio and television. On a newspaper or magazine, the editor or publisher may do the writing. Or, there may be an editorial writer. In the case of large publications, there could be an editorial board. The point is that *they* do the writing. You can't write an editorial for them, as you would a news release for the news side, and expect to have it published.

Your approach, if you have material that seems to you worthy of editorial page consideration, would be to ask your regular news-feature contact for background on who writes the editorials, how receptive he or they are to outside suggestions, and how to submit an idea or material to them. Then, make an appointment.

When you visit the editor, tell him why you believe your organization deserves his editorial support, and bring along written material that may help him. You may find that the preparation of a fact sheet might be the best way to organize basic information. In the case of an important anniversary, a list of historic dates and a description of outstanding projects carried out through the years would be valuable. If you are looking for editorial support for a fund drive, or greater community understanding of an outstanding project, assemble not only the factual details, but go into the thinking behind the project and the objectives. And be prepared to answer questions or to provide further information. Offer to make your president, or other well-informed individuals, available for a question-and-answer session, if such interest is indicated.

If an editorial writer wants to dig out information firsthand, by all means invite him to attend any meeting you have scheduled on the subject, or set up any special meeting he may suggest.

Some newspapers run "guest editorials." These usually are reserved for very special occasions and therefore are rare. The invitation to contribute a guest editorial normally would originate with the newspaper. But you could plant the idea for such an invitation if you have a qualified and articulate expert to prepare such an editorial.

Opportunities for editorial comment in electronic media are

even rarer. However, you may be familiar, for example, with the CBS editorial comment at the end of some news programs and the "Editorial Reply" segment at the end of others. For what opportunities may be available to you, watch and listen to the television and radio stations serving your community.

There is need for caution in this area. Sometimes editorials praise; sometimes they criticize. However, if there is criticism, and it's constructive criticism, you still will benefit.

Letters to the Editor

Under a variety of headings, many newspapers publish letters from readers, usually on the editorial page. They give such names to this section as Vox Pop, The Cracker Barrel, Our Readers Write, Dear Editor, or just plain Letters to the Editor.

You should consider a letter to the editor as another way

— to call attention to an upcoming event

— to call attention to a worthy cause

— to enlist support for a matter of vital public concern

— to explain a misunderstood point

— to take a stand

— to thank the community for its support

— to thank individuals or a group for some special service.

In the latter category could be an open letter of thanks to the volunteer firemen who put out a grass fire that threatened your headquarters, or an open letter of thanks to the canvassers who made your fund drive a success.

Depending on the content, a letter to the editor should be signed by the president of your organization, or by the general membership chairman, in the case of a membership drive, or by whoever is best qualified by authority or background to present the communication. You may prepare the letter as a part of your publicity role, but normally you would not sign it.

Obviously, you'll never write a letter to the editor to complain about lack of cooperation or to call attention to a misquotation or factual mistake in a news story. If an error is significant or damaging, talk it over first with your regular news-feature contact. He may have a suggestion that will solve the problem—not create a new one. Your job is to win friends with the press—so play it cool and be reasonable if you have a complaint.

A letter to the editor should be used in a positive way to benefit your organization and to project it as a good citizen and a community asset.

Working with Clergymen

Don't overlook clergymen as a possible source of support for your organization's projects, whether spiritual, charitable or of other important community interest. Good causes often win special mentions from the pulpit. If you have a project that supports what a church is doing, and you know it is customary to talk about such things from the pulpit, see what you can do to win support. As with an editorial writer, take along a fact sheet and any other information particularly appropriate for the church.

Capitalizing on Your Results

Getting publicity is only part of your job. What you do with it after you get it can be highly rewarding. As the golfer knows, it is the follow-through that gives the extra distance and final measure of control.

Most of what follows represents good internal public relations, but often is neglected.

The Clipping Book

Keep a clipping book to display your publicity results. This is a simple, basic tool, but it has three valuable purposes:

1. As a composite record of the organization's accomplishments, it should impress your people with the value of what they are doing and create a greater willingness to continue or augment their support.

2. It is a constantly growing addition to the archives.

3. It will help your successor.

It can also be a valuable means in selling your organization on an expanded publicity program—that is, persuading it to provide a more adequate budget—and interesting others to help.

A clipping book might be kept up by your historian, if you have one. If not, some other member may be willing to help. It should not be a cheap paste-pot-and-scissors production, but a proud presentation in a good quality cover and on good quality stock . . . something that will impress an outsider.

A clipping book shouldn't be limited to the stories that have appeared in newspapers or magazines. It should include a background introduction to each project. It may call for an interesting explanation in a typewritten "box." And you shouldn't hesitate to use prints of any appropriate photographs— regardless of whether they've been published. If you have a radio program placement and can get a transcript, put that in your clipping book. If you are fortunate enough to make a television placement, you should have both a photographic and a transcript record of the event. If a major speech is made and a text is available, put it in your book. Build up the record every way you can. If you tape record a speech or an interview, the tape should go into the archives—but a typed copy or highlight excerpts should go into the clipping book.

Bulletin Boards

If your organization has its own facilities, perhaps it has a bulletin board in the reception hall. If so, make a habit of posting publicity results as they become available. A good technique is to have a section of the bulletin board assigned to you. You can create a headline for it, such as "We're in the Spotlight" or "We're in the News." Keep changing your exhibits as frequently as you can. Get your members in the habit of expecting something new whenever they look at the board.

Special Displays

For your annual meeting, a banquet, an open house, or a tour, develop a special display of publicity results. This could be on a bulletin board, or on sets of easels, if the quantity of exhibits justifies. You could sectionalize the exhibits by project, if you have multiple projects. For a meeting of your membership, you might present the background story on how the articles they saw in the paper came about.

For any kind of an exhibit, photographs will be a must. Here is the extra payoff for you if, in your regular news and feature work, you are able to obtain a good supply of pictures.

Slides

If you are able to take 35mm color photographs in your regular work, you will find them invaluable for developing a slide show for your annual meeting. Give the presidential report extra impact by highlighting the year's events. Slides can be utilized also in special projectors for viewing when you have an open house, or are trying to interest prospective members in your organization.

The Club Bulletin

The club bulletin (or news letter), if your organization has one, probably will have its own editor. However, you should contribute material to it—both stories and photographs. A background feature on how an interview was arranged, or how some other project was carried out that made headlines, should be worthwhile. Pictures you have taken undoubtedly will be very much appreciated.

Miscellaneous

If you have a headquarters building, give it a frank appraisal. Is your organization putting its best foot forward? Is your sign out front shabby? Do you need a new one? What face do you present to a visitor . . . to a passer-by?

Don't forget letters of thanks—to people who were interviewed, to speakers, to anyone who made a substantial contribution to your organization's program. These are not the public letters of thanks mentioned earlier in the section on "Letters to the Editor," but private letters. In some cases, you should draft them for your president; in some cases, as a letter to an editor thanking him for his special attention, you could be the signer.

Finally, in things to do, sit down with your president and/or program chairman and go over what you are doing, what other organizations are doing, what problems you have met in trying to place publicity. If your program is not worth writing about, try to invest it with the life it needs to be attractive to the community. Manufacture some events that will draw public attention. Try to contribute some creative input. If there are no headlines, do your best to see that there will be. More than anyone else in your organization, you will know just what the outside world thinks of it—and what needs to be done to lift up its image.

VIII HANDLING PERSONAL AND FAMILY PUBLICITY

Once the word gets around that you've been having success in "getting pieces in the paper," brace yourself for requests from colleagues, friends and relatives to place stories for them. You may be story material yourself—or you may see a story worth doing in your family, in your neighborhood, among your friends, or in business.

Don't look on these as "chores." If you establish a reputation with your publicity outlets as a source of worthwhile news and interesting features, you will be appreciated—and your efforts will enhance the relationship you are trying to build with the press for your organization's publicity assignment.

In the handling of personal and family publicity, the studies you've made of your outlets, and your talks with your news-feature contacts, should guide you on what is acceptable. For special deadlines or requirements—and there are those, especially for engagement and wedding stories—ask your regular press contacts whom to call or, on your own, call the society editors or the women's page editors.

You will hear, time and again, that "names make news." Personal and family publicity is just that—names. However, definitions of what constitutes news vary. The village weekly still will run an item on a resident's visit to the big city, but some big-city newspapers won't even run a wedding story unless it is paid for.

LAYMAN'S PUBLICITY GUIDE

Family Events

Engagements and weddings lead the list of newsmakers, and newspapers with "society pages" usually have a special day on which they publish the bulk of the engagement and wedding announcements.

Your first duty will be to learn what the deadlines are for photographs and for story material, and what special requirements there are both for the kind of picture and the story information. As noted earlier, some big-city newspapers won't run a wedding story unless it is paid for—but even when you pay, there are limitations and requirements. Other big-city newspapers have qualifications that must be met. There would be no trouble getting a story in if the family of the bride or groom is in the Social Register, for example. But there would be no chance whatever if no one, in either family, met the newspaper's special qualifications.

In the average community, however, whether served by a daily or a weekly (or both), you will find that announcements of engagements and wedding stories are important local news. Just find out when the material must be in the publication's hands, and in what form. You'll find sample engagement and wedding releases on pages 133 and 134, but be guided also by what your editors tell you.

Society page stories read pretty much alike. Your challenge in preparing one, therefore, is to seek out every bit of information of special interest. If the bride traces her ancestry back to Pochahontas, that's a part of your story. Don't stop with the bride and groom and their families in your search for interesting information. Canvass the guest list also. It may contain distinguished names worthy of mention. The bride's gown may be an heirloom of historic interest.

Birth announcements, if published at all by a newspaper, usually are just simple factual announcements of the new arrivals. However, if there is information of unusual interest, put it in your story.

Christenings also usually are just simple factual announcements. But, again, information of unusual interest may warrant a news story and, in some circumstances, a picture will be indicated if the parents or members of their families are distinguished figures. Normally, a christening that would be considered a big news event would be covered by a publication's own staff.

Wedding anniversaries are newsmakers when they mark the big ones—particularly the 50th. The observance of such an anniversary may be covered with a picture and caption. However, if enough is made of the occasion, it may call for an accompanying story. It depends on who the principals are and how much is made of the occasion that determine what you should do. Usually a photograph and brief story will suffice.

Birthdays qualify for newspaper space only in exceptional circumstances. Anyone reaching 100 years will call for special attention and usually an interview if the person has an active mind and interesting recollections. Normally, a newspaper would assign one of its staff for an interview and a photograph. Below the 100-year-mark, interest tapers off—but a 90-year-old or a 95-year-old looking back on a distinguished career, or the changes in town, or just reminiscing could make a worthwhile feature. A special birthday party, or a special birthday cake, anything with an unusual twist could make a story. But don't rule out youngsters as possibilities. The child you had as a mascot for your Heart Fund Drive may be good copy again when she celebrates a birthday in good health. On birthdays there is only one hard-and-fast rule—ignore them unless they're special. And if there's a good story, don't forget photographs.

Family reunions are news only if they have some special distinction. A group of brothers and sisters meeting for the first time since they parted as teen-agers in a foreign land could make an interesting story. An every-year reunion of a local family that never strayed far from the area conceivably would not be news until the reunions reached a significant number, such as the 25th. Again, as in all the foregoing, search for the unusual. If you think you're on the trail of a good story, but aren't sure how to proceed, call your press contacts. They may counsel you to go ahead, or to forget it, or they may want to provide their own coverage.

Trips. So many people travel these days, on business or for pleasure, that the old-time "personal," reporting goings and comings of local residents, is all but forgotten, except in small communities. If you have publicity outlets that are still receptive to personals, contribute what you can. If they are not receptive, nevertheless keep your eyes open for the unusual. A local resident's three-week tourist holiday in England may not be worth a line, but if something special happened on the tour which is of public interest, that is a different matter. The distinction here is between personal interest and public interest. If there is something about a trip that interests you as an outsider, chances are that it may have the ingredients for a story that will interest others.

Educational

Educational institutions generally have professional publicity staffs whose jobs include sending news about students to their home-town newspapers. Thus you may read regularly in your local publications about students who have just made the Dean's List. You may also read about who has been appointed to the Student Council, who has made the Varsity in football, and at graduation time, who was graduated with what degree and with what special honors.

Thus, there is nothing for you to do *unless* a student from your family or neighborhood is attending a school which is not servicing news to your newspapers.

On the other hand, if there is no organized school coverage, the field is open for you. Anyone making the Dean's List is worth an item, as often as the new Dean's List is posted. Other scholastic achievements are newsworthy, too. And in sports, any student making a team, winning special acclaim, earning a letter, or being elected a captain or manager, deserves a story. At graduation, if there are many graduates from your community, usually a listing is all you will find in your newspapers. If you have names to submit, do so, but confine your item to the brief information printed about others—unless there is some special reason for doing more.

Class reunions, like anniversaries, usually depend on age for news interest. A reunion of last year's high school graduating class may be fun for the participants but means little to the editor. On the other hand, the 50th anniversary of a class, if the reunion is well attended from far and near, would be worth a photograph and a story. The 10th, the 25th, these too are possibilities, if the principals are interesting or the program offers something unusual.

Military

The military services, like educational institutions, have publicity staffs who send news to the home-town newspapers of promotions received by servicemen.

However, there may be stories for you to write when a serviceman is selected for a special detail in a public ceremony or notable event, or is otherwise involved in something that has attracted public interest. A serviceman may write to his parents, for example, about an unusual assignment and the parents may give you the information.

Business

The business world is filled with personal news—new jobs, promotions, awards, patent grants, elections, speeches, convention activities, etc.

The larger corporations, with professional publicity staffs, strive to do a thorough job in servicing local media with all appropriate news. They leave little for you to do. However, smaller businesses usually do not have publicity facilities, and co-workers, friends or relatives in such businesses may appreciate your help in getting news coverage when events warrant.

For a detailed outline of the numerous opportunities in this field, see Chapter IX—Small Business Publicity—and particularly the section entitled "People Are News."

Personal Publicity

A neighbor, a friend, a relative, or you yourself may be newsworthy in other ways than through activities and occasions already discussed.

An unusual hobby, the more unusual the better, will make an interesting feature. Outline the facts to your news-feature contact on the publication that does the best job on features. He may suggest that you go ahead and develop it yourself or take it up with his editors and decide on staff coverage. If it is you and your hobby that are to be featured, obviously the publication should develop the story. But you should be able to give it good guidance.

Other potential newsmakers are honors or awards, special achievements, etc. Prize awards, as a rule, are publicized by the awarding organization, and need not concern you.

Generally, there is standard acceptance of some kinds of news (such as a student making the Dean's List) and a great field of opportunity where there is something unusual. Educate your nose to sniff out the unusual—and you're bound to find potential reader interest.

IX   SMALL-BUSINESS PUBLICITY

Perhaps you run a local business—but this handbook has come to your attention because you are involved also in a community organization. And you ask yourself whether it might serve also as a do-it-yourself guide for a small business whose limited news-making activities or limited budget do not permit the hiring of professional publicity services.

Yes, it can!

True, this guide was designed primarily for community groups and organizations, but the principles and operations of publicity are the same for a business as for a community group. However, there is one essential difference: the community group usually is a nonprofit organization; the businessman is in business for profit. Therefore, the media (newspapers, radio, television, magazines) look upon him through different spectacles. Whether they view you as a potential advertiser, they recognize that your basic outlook is commercial and not unselfish.

Why and when and where you as a businessman advertise are beyond the scope of this guide—but regardless of whether you advertise, there are opportunities in publicity you should explore.

Why Publicity Is Valuable

As large, successful companies have found, it is good business for a company to talk about its business when it has something of interest to say to the public.

- It is good business for a company with respect to its customers, because they prefer to do business with a company they know—and know as a *good* company.

- It is useful with respect to employees—and prospective employees—because they like to work for a company that has a good image in the community.

- It makes a contribution to relations with its owners, because favorable publicity enhances its standing in the marketplace—and hence, its attractiveness as an investment.

- It is good business for a company with respect to the community wherein it operates, because community goodwill is a precious asset; it is valuable for a company to be recognized as "a good citizen."

And it is good for the media to present news and features about local businesses, because these enterprises are community assets and good news about them is a reflection of the commercial strength of the community.

But First, Some Cautions

Before getting into how you can decide on a publicity program for your business, here are three cautions:

First, if you advertise, don't try to use your advertising "clout" to get "free" space in the news columns.

It is done. Some publications, in fact, not only accept such pressure, but actually solicit it. Some offer a certain amount of editorial visibility in return for a given amount of advertising.

But the main editorial thrust is to judge news—from whatever source—on the basis of whether it is bona fide reader/subscriber news. If you have news of genuine interest, it will be used because it is news—and it will get readership of positive value to you. If it is a "puff" article, it will be recognized as such by readers if it is printed, and you will probably either gain nothing or lose ground. So, advertiser or non-advertiser, your best route in dealing with the press is to present your material for judgment purely on its objective news and interest values.

Secondly, if you expect to have good relations with a publication over the long term, remember that you are on a two-way street. You have information that you would like to see published; a publication has the responsibility of trying to get as much information as it can for completeness and reader interest. Therefore, be prepared to answer questions, either when you approach a publication or when it approaches you. Be as helpful as you can within the limits of what you can reasonably divulge, and be as tactful as you can when you must draw the line. But even in the event of bad news—a tragic accident in a plant, for example—you should still be as cooperative as you can. Be available; be communicative; be courteous.

Thirdly, if your company is publicly held (owned, that is, by outside investors) and financial information is to be a part of your publicity output, be aware of the fact that the Securities Exchange Commission has definite regulations regarding corporate news releases that may affect the value of securities. The SEC is adamant about prompt and full disclosure. To find out what you can do, and must do, in the specialized financial area, start by getting the guidelines published by the New York Stock Exchange or other exchanges.

As to the other publicity avenues you should explore, much of what follows will apply more to an industrial organization—particularly a manufacturing plant. But whether you're a butcher, a baker or a candlestick maker, there may be opportunities which you can capitalize.

Size of business, per se, is no criterion. A nurseryman who is an articulate authority on gardening may find his advice valued in the gardening section of his local newspaper. The small-business donor of a scholarship may generate periodic publicity for an activity having nothing to do with his business, but reflecting favorably upon it, nevertheless.

How Do You Begin?

If you want to find out whether you should consider a publicity program for your business, or whether you should skip it, the best way to begin is to take an inventory of your potential.

At one extreme, you may find that there is so little of outside interest in your organization that a publicity effort would hardly be worth the investment of time and money.

At the other extreme, you may be agreeably surprised by the number of opportunities your business offers for publicity, both in activities already going on and in projects you can create.

In addition, inventory taking can point up the *kind* of a program your activities can or should support.

So, to answer the question of how to begin, here is a step-by-step program. These steps, by the way, are not to be considered one at a time in isolation with front vision only, but with bits of side vision here and there, looking at each within the context of the whole.

1. *Check the checklists.* Look over the checklists in the next section of this chapter, and see what there is in them that applies to your operation. Also, what new projects you might generate to develop publicity. If your ammunition is scanty, don't get into the battle. But if you believe you have something to support a program, go on to the next step.

2. *Determine your publicity outlets.* Begin by reading the section on the media in Chapter III.

   To find out what publications serve your area which you may not be aware of, go to your public library and consult the current edition of the *Ayer Directory of Publications.*

Start with your own community's listing, just to be sure something doesn't exist that you don't happen to know about. Then, according to the way trade flows in your general area, look up nearby communities and those in your general area, such as in your county or in your part of your county.

Study them all. If your library has a file, fine. If not, buy copies of those you don't regularly receive and take the trouble to read them over a period of a few weeks to see what attention they give to business and industry.

Some dailies, for example, have one day a week when they devote a part of a page to photographs and announcements of men and women promoted to new positions or joining a local organization. By checking such dailies, you will see what kind of space they give to local business and industry and, for your later deadline background, when. A little homework can be very revealing.

The weeklies also should have your attention, including shopper giveaways which emphasize community news. In many cases, their staffs are small and they welcome news contributions.

If you are a very small business in a big city, and the publication outlets are only big ones, you obviously have little opportunity for local publicity. If you're in New York City, you're not going to crack *The New York Times* unless you have something unusual, and that would be a rare one-shot.

While at the library to check publications, you can find out what other directories are available, particularly in two other fields—radio and television, and trade publications.

Trade publications can be of important value to you if, aside from what you may want to do locally to build a community image, you want to develop a good image before others in your line of business. For example, if you are a manufac-turer who produces new designs or new products or specializes in new ideas, your trade image is exceedingly important in itself and it can be used to enhance your local image.

Chances are that you're familiar with the trade publications serving your field. But, again, just to be sure that something doesn't exist that you ought to know about, take a look in the library at *Standard Rate & Data's* latest issue on trade publications, and also the *Ayer Directory of Publications.* They break down the publications by the fields they serve, so it is very simple to check over the category in which your business is classified. Not only that, S.R.&D. will tell you the make-up of the audience of each publication and usually give a summary of the editorial content. There would be no point, for example, in sending new product releases and photographs to a publication which lacks a new product section. Thus, you save yourself time and money when you determine what outlets there are that reach the audiences you want to reach, and what kinds of material they will accept.

Standard Rate & Data also publishes similar information on radio and television stations, and you should explore its listings if you believe you have material of interest to the electronic media.

Let's suppose, however, that your local library does not have those references. Then, go to your nearest big-city library or to a local advertising agency.

3. *Determine your objectives.* Having assured yourself by Steps 1 and 2 that there is news material in your organiza-tion of interest to outsiders, and that there are media that accept such material, you should decide what aims you'd like to accomplish. Is a better community image one of your

goals? Are you trying to reach local customers? Do you want to make a good impression on the people in the field you are in? Is an enhanced standing with your employees your main objective? Or are you looking for a blend of some or all these?

4. *Draw up a definite program.* Now that you're aware of the kind of publicity potential you have, the market for such information, and what you'd like to accomplish by means of this visibility, you are ready to put the pieces together into an action program. It should spell out the specifics of what you are going to do—and when. Obviously, new appointments can be announced only when new appointments are made, so here you can decide only on the "what" and let the "when" take care of itself. But if there is an open house, or an anniversary celebration, or an awards dinner in your future, pinpoint it on your publicity calendar. In your action program, you should include a budget. Photography costs money. Dinners cost money—for the dinners themselves, the invitations, the awards, etc. If you don't know what photographs cost, ask your local newspaper for the names of photographers who provide good news pictures, and make a few calls for estimates. If you don't know what your dinner budget should call for, contact a hotel or motel that caters to group celebrations and get an estimate. Your blueprint for publicity action, thus, should include the activities you propose to undertake and a worksheet of estimated costs.

5. *Decide on who is to do the job.* Who is going to carry out your program? You? If you have a very small organization, there may be no one but you. Take a candid look at what talent you may have "in-house"—and also whether that talent can be spared. It takes time to woo contacts, to work on special events, to do the writing, to supervise the photography, and to deliver the finished product. A small

program of occasional routine press releases could be handled simply by yourself, with your secretary doing the typing and making a few phone calls. But the more ambitious you are, the more time and talent and money will be needed.

6. *Hire outside help?* If you have good publicity potential and are eager to capitalize on it, and if your budget permits, think about supplementing your in-house talents with a free-lance publicity expert or part-time help of a publicity organization. Either of them would be glad to take over the whole assignment, for a fee. But the more you can do for yourself, the less this outside help has to do—and the cost obviously will be less. It should be acknowledged, however, that outside help, intelligently used, can be a time- and money-saver, if the special requirements of your program warrant enlisting such services.

7. *Go to work.* To implement your action program, follow the guidelines in preceding chapters on how to work with the media, on what to write, on how to write, and on the role of photography. Some things will be easy and others will be difficult, but a well-planned and well-executed publicity program will yield definite values of benefit to you in your business.

One project to tackle first is the preparation of a fact sheet or fact book about your organization. It can be as simple as a single sheet of paper, or a small booklet of mimeographed or multilithed pages, or a printed brochure, but it should cover the salient facts about your enterprise—what it makes or does; when it started; how big it is; who its key executives are. Such a background document will help introduce you when you make calls on the press, and it can be left for reference. As a part of good public relations practice, copies also should be left in your reception room to help introduce you to salesmen and other visitors. (For patterns, see the sample fact sheets on pages 156 and 158.)

Publicity Checklists

News in business and industry comes from what has been described as "the four P's"—people, plant, products and programs. We might add a fifth "P," public service. These are attractive categories, but perhaps over-simplified and therefore a little difficult in all situations. People you have, of course, but instead of a plant you may have a retail establishment; instead of products you may have services; and programs may seem to be a little vague and hard to fit into the mold. Public service is an area open to everyone.

Therefore, for what there may be in your business that constitutes news, and what you can undertake if you want to make news, here is a multiple checklist arranged a little differently, though basically meeting the requirements of the four or five "P's."

This is strictly a series of "what' listings—without the "how to." It will include speeches as newsmaking activities, but will not venture to tell you how to make an effective speech; it will include the open house as a newsmaking activity, but will not tell you how to stage one; it will mention many other activities which are good newsmakers, without telling you how to conduct them. The "how to," when it comes to giving the detail of planning and executing newsmaking events, is beyond the scope of this guide. But don't neglect the "how to"—the success of an event depends upon it.

People Are News

A prime producer of acceptable news is recognition of individuals. The old newspaper principle is, "Names make news," and here are happenings where you can name names:

- Company elections—board of directors; officers (See sample release on page 155.)

- Major executive changes

- Organizational changes—new departments; new titles

- Appointments

- Awards—recognizing
  - achievement
  - contest winners (incentive program winners)
  - merit
  - safety records
  - service
  - suggestions for product or operations improvement

- Anniversaries (people, not company)

  (awarding of buttons, pins, or other emblems honoring service milestones, such as 5-year, 10-year, 25-year, 50-year service)

- Honors . . . from
  - educational institutions
  - government
  - organizations—local, national, international
  - professional societies

- Participation in

  community activities

  political activities

  professional society activities

- Patents or inventions

- Retirements

- Employee speeches or other presentations

- Sports sponsored by the company for employees or outside organizations

- Unusual hobbies

- Distinguished visitors

- Deaths

A note on conventions: There is so much convention travel these days that a convention seldom qualifies as a newsworthy item—unless a speech of wide interest or an award is involved. If there is news, security needs for the homes of the newsmaking persons dictate that you do not announce absences in advance. If Mr. and Mrs. Peter Jolly win an incentive award trip to Bermuda, tell about it after they've returned home. Publicity should be designed to be good for all concerned—except thieves who read the newspapers for helpful tips.

News in the Physical Establishment

Business expansion is good news and therefore offers fertile publicity opportunities.

The construction of a major new facility, for example, contains the material for a long succession of good copy, including

- the original announcement of the planned expansion, perhaps when a new site is acquired

- the unveiling of the architect's rendering and explanation of the design

- the awarding of the contract

- the ground-breaking

- the laying of the cornerstone
- progress reports as major portions of the over-all project are completed
- the "topping out" ceremony
- the dedication
- the formal opening
- open houses, perhaps separate ones for different groups—employees and their families; the community; customers; other special audiences.

A major project will command major attention, but even a small expansion can be utilized to some extent for beneficial publicity.

Newsworthy physical-establishment developments include:

Purchase of site for expansion

New construction—new buildings or additions

Modernization of existing facilities

Purchase of new facilities

Acquisition of another company or a company line

Installation of new production equipment

Installation of new safety devices

Installation of anti-pollution systems or techniques to better the environment

Branching out into another community

Celebration of a plant anniversary

News in Company Operations

Recognition of people in an organization makes one kind of news; developments dealing with the physical plant itself create opportunity for another kind of news; while a third source of news is the operations of the company.

In this operations area are:

New products

New services

New processes

Research developments or discoveries

Organizational changes

Safety records or achievements

Safety programs

New production records

Unusual shipments (the largest, the heaviest, the fastest, the millionth, the first or the last, etc.)

Receipt of contracts (military orders, big orders, unusual orders)

Use of company product on an eventful occasion (such as special equipment on space missions)

Industry recognition of a company achievement

Special surveys or studies

Special exhibits or displays

On the negative side, a company will find itself in the news through accidents, deaths, reductions in work force, fire, flood, pollution, labor controversy, etc. Bad news is unfortunate, but salvage out of it what you can by being as cooperative as you possibly can. You may prevent a bad situation from becoming worse, and good press relations for times of good news will be enhanced.

Ideas for Special Events and Occasions

To review some of the foregoing material and present it in a different perspective, here is an idea list for special events and special occasions.

Anniversaries

1. Anniversary of a company's founding. Public interest can be attracted to the major milestones—such as the 10th, 25th, 50th and 100th anniversaries—but annual "in-house" celebrations could be considered or an annual dinner or other get-together for retired employees or for a Family Night.

2. Anniversary of the company's founder (75th birthday and still going strong, for example) or a significant service anniversary of a company leader or worker.

3. The anniversary of a product or process. There are two kinds of opportunities here. You can mark a company event, such as the 25th anniversary of your first widget or the introduction of the special process you developed which made your company famous. Or you can mark an industry event which is being celebrated generally. For example, if you make transistors and a significant milestone in transistor history is being observed by an industry association, you can key in with your own anniversary project. Or, even if there is an industry anniversary you think ought to be celebrated, but no one does anything about it, you can still use it as the reason for staging a localized event.

4. The anniversary of the opening of a plant or other major facility.

5. The anniversary of an important branch or major extension of a business into a new field.

6. Anniversary of a company's entrance into the community.

Open houses

Open houses usually are held to unveil a new facility or to entertain special groups, often when a plant is not in operation. There may be exhibits, displays or demonstrations; there may be a short information program; there may be entertainment; and suitably identified company personnel to act as hosts and to answer possible questions are an important asset.

Open houses should be considered as worthwhile projects in a number of situations, including:

1. To mark the opening of a new plant or office or wing.

2. On completion of major remodeling.

3. The celebration of an anniversary.

4. On announcement of a major new product or process.

5. When special new facilities are installed (such as anti-pollution, new technologies, etc.)

6. As part of an over-all industry salute to the community.

7. When appropriate to the special observance of a day, week or month being celebrated locally or in the state or nation. (Check the news almanac listings of special days and weeks proclaimed in state and nation; watch your newspapers and trade magazines for announcements of local proclamations and special industry promotions.)

8. To mark a special achievement in production—a record, an unusual number (as the millionth unit), an industry award, etc.

9. As a part of any community visitation program.

10. For employee families; employee organizations (25-Year-Club); retired employees.

LAYMAN'S PUBLICITY GUIDE

Plant tours
──────────

A plant tour may be a part of an open house, but often is not. Guests at an open house may see a new facility, hear a short program, have refreshments in a large assembly room, but not get into the operating plant proper. If visitors are to trek through the plant when it is operating (unless safety hazards or noise pose special problems) they should have qualified guides. Guides may be assigned to small parties, explaining as they go along and answering questions that come up. Or they may be assigned to stations, giving their explanations as groups move along a well-marked route from station to station. Exhibits, displays and demonstrations suitable for an open house are equally suitable as techniques for a plant tour.

Here are some audiences for whom plant tours may be considered:

1. For the press—in connection with a newsworthy event or announcement. Even if only one reporter is your audience, take the time to plan the tour carefully to bring out the most interesting information and background in the least possible time. Don't just embark on "a walk through the plant" which may wear him out and bore him to death.

2. For any interested visitor, perhaps a regular "Welcome to Visitors" once a day at a certain time; once a week on a certain day; once a month; or even once a year—however you want to set it up when guides can be made available. Trained guides are a must.

3. For students—for special-study classes in the field of your business; for grade or high school classes generally, to broaden their education and develop their community appreciation; and for college students, perhaps during a school-term vacation, as a part of your recruiting program.

4. For employee families; employee organizations; retired employees.

5. For community groups—church groups, service clubs, senior citizens, youth organizations.

6. For special-interest groups, such as members of professional societies, particularly if there is a specially proclaimed day or week honoring them, and you are important in their field of endeavor.

7. For special groups of outsiders—a trade delegation visiting your community; delegates attending a local convention; patrons and exhibitors from an industry trade show.

Ceremonies

1. Dedication of a new building.

2. Dedication of new facilities or new equipment.

3. Dedication of a park or recreation area.

4. Unveiling of a historical marker or commemorative plaque.

5. Ground-breaking for new construction.

6. Laying a corner stone.

7. Topping out a new structure.

8. Awarding a scholarship, a medal, a prize, an honor.

Your Company and the Community

Besides the news of outside interest your company may generate—through your people, your establishment, the developments and achievements of your day-to-day operations, and special events—there are many other things you can do and say in the important area of building your community image.

How much of an economic factor is your company in the community?

If you have a good story to tell about your expenditures in the community, your payroll, the taxes you pay, your efforts to help other industry in your area, or your efforts to better the environment and benefit the ecology, you should find ways to tell it.

As a good citizen, you perform the usual good deeds of good citizens—but what specifically can you do to gain greater recognition?

Many community activities in which you are or may become involved are the usual activities of community-minded citizens. What you do will speak for itself through the publicity gained by the sponsoring organizations—such as service on a community committee, leadership in a charitable fund drive, etc.—and the respect won from your fellow participants. But should you stop there?

Here is a short list of some things you can do besides "ordinary" participation in the work of the many organizations that flourish in your community for business, social, charitable, religious, or educational reasons. Some, on the face of things, will not achieve visibility in the press—but that will not matter. In a good cause, you still will enjoy the benefit of having exposed some audience . . . some group . . . some individuals . . . to the good things you are doing—and you will have contributed to the favorable impressions which, in total, constitute your public image.

Here are some ideas on what you can do:

1. Provide a speaker or program material for a business club luncheon or other community function. First, get in touch with the program chairman or member of the program committee of each community group that has a need for informative programs, or special interest in the kind of information you can present. Find out what the program schedule is—and where there are holes to be filled. Then, make an offer to "put on a show" that will be interesting and appropriate to your audience, and a valid reward for your public relations effort.

2. Look for opportunities to present your story to school groups, through speeches or demonstrations, before school classes or assemblies, as well as special tours through your facilities for grade school, high school or college groups.

3. Work with local clergymen and the heads of clubs and groups in churches to set up programs—speeches or tours—for their calendars.

4. Work with youth groups (and senior citizen groups) on appropriate projects. If there is some part of your operation that is particularly pertinent to a Boy Scout or Girl Scout interest, for example, set up a little program or demonstration.

5. In any fund drive—for a hospital or organized charity or other nonprofit institution—consider a special contribution: a bed, a window, special equipment, etc. Or, see whether your employees are interested in doing something different (dolls for the children, something special for the handicapped), and encourage them with ideas and other support.

6. If you have an auditorium, conference room or other facility suitable for a community activity on a regular or special basis, consider making it available.

7. Other than the usual things that might occur to you in the foregoing, make your facilities available for an indoor or outdoor art show, if the location is convenient for the desired crowd and the facilities appropriate for the purpose.

8. If you have extra land for future expansion, consider making it available on a temporary basis—that is, until you may need it—for a local ball field or playground.

9. In the field of education, the awarding of scholarships

yields good publicity. In the field of sports, sponsor a team.

10. Make an observation (or be interviewed) on a local economic problem.

11. Organize (or sponsor) a roundtable, luncheon, dinner, or special meeting for local opinion leaders on a prime matter of current local business concern.

12. Make a comment (or be interviewed) on a matter of state, national, even international interest. This depends upon the nature of your business and the breadth of your involvement. It depends also upon your ability to put something important into words.

This list is only an indication, by way of examples, of what you can do if you use your ingenuity. Many other possibilities should occur to you on candid evaluation of your resources and your goals, as well as creative appraisal of your opportunities.

X   THE MATTER OF STYLE

There is no universal style observed by all publications. Some, in writing about the government in Washington, D.C., style it the "Federal government," with a capital "F." Some style it the "federal government," with a lower case "f." Some use two capitals—"Federal Government."

In your publicity releases, if you are writing for only one newspaper, copy its style. If you are writing for many, you won't be able to wholly please them all. But you can please most of them by observing the style rules that follow because these are the rules the majority of newspapers observe.

Capitalization

Newspapers generally follow a "down style"—that is, they are more sparing in their use of capital letters than organizations and companies, especially in titles. Thus: Capitalize a title when it precedes a personal name. Lowercase a title standing alone or following a name. (Exception: President is always capitalized for the incumbent President of the United States.)

Executive Secretary Clark Blanchard of the Community Center . . .

Clark Blanchard, executive secretary of the Community Center . . .

The executive secretary said in his annual report . . .

Capitalize holidays, historic events, ecclesiastical feasts, fast days, special events, etc.

Mother's Day; New Year's Day; National Safety Week

Capitalize specific regions.

Midwest; Southern California; Chicago's near *South Side*

Capitalize party names for political parties—but not the word "party." Capitalize party members.

Democratic party; He is a Republican

Some proper names that have acquired independent common meaning are not capitalized.

paris green; dutch door; brussels sprouts

Names

Spell the name of a person as he or she uses it.

Gregg du Pont; Winston R. Du Pont; Bruce F. Dupont

Omit the comma when Jr., Sr., or Roman numerals are used to differentiate male members of a family with identical names.

John Smith III is the nephew of John Smith Jr.

A married woman has the title of Mrs. followed by her husband's name. Exceptions are stage and sports stars, and other notables with names well established in the public eye.

The full name of a man is used when he is first mentioned in a release; thereafter use the title of Mr. followed by the last name, unless he has a distinctive title. Exceptions include historic figures (such as George Washington or Abraham Lincoln), sports figures and convicted criminals or persons of unsavory reputation. The title of Mr. is never used with the full name of a man in his first mention in a release.

Use the abbreviations below for titles only when they are used before full names. When they are used before last names only, the titles must be spelled out.

Gov.—Governor

Lt. Gov.—Lieutenant Governor

Sen.—Senator

Rep.—Representative

Prof.—Professor

Supt.—Superintendent

Do not abbreviate the following titles at any time: General Manager; Secretary-General; Secretary-Treasurer; President; Secretary; Treasurer; Vice President, etc. They are capitalized only when used before names.

In military titles, use abbreviations, except for the rank of Commodore. Thus, for the Army, Gen., Maj. Gen., Col., Maj., Capt., Lt., Pfc., etc. In the Navy and Coast Guard, Adm., RAdm., Cmdr. for Commander, Lt., Lt. (j.g.); Ens., etc. Seaman also is spelled out. Air Force commissioned officers are abbreviated the same as the Army's. Non-commissioned designations include MSgt. for Master Sergeant, Airman 1.C. for Airman 1st Class and Airman for Airman Basic.

Religious

In general, when writing of clergymen, write: the Rev. John Smith, the Rev. Mr. Smith, the Rev. Dr. John Jones, Dr. Jones. Do not use Rev. without "the" preceding it.

Roman Catholic usage: The Rev. John Smith, Father Smith; the Rt. Rev. Msgr. John Jones, Msgr. Jones; the Most Rev. John Jones, bishop of the Denver diocese, Bishop Jones; Francis Cardinal Spellman, Cardinal Spellman.

Episcopal usage: A deacon or priest is referred to as the Rev. John Jones or the Rev. Mr. Jones. A dean is the Very Rev. John

Jones, the Rev. Mr. Jones, or Dean Jones. A bishop is the Rt. Rev. John Jones, the Rev. Mr. Jones or Bishop Jones.

Jewish usage: Rabbi James Wise, Rabbi Wise, Dr. Wise. Cantor Harry Epstein, Cantor Epstein.

Christian Science usage: Practitioner, Lecturer, Reader. Do not use Reverend in any form.

Methodist usage: Pastor, Minister, Preacher, Bishop. Mr. with surname is acceptable.

Lutheran usage: Pastor John Jones, Pastor Jones, Mr. Jones.

Latter-Day Saint (Mormon) usage: President Spencer Kimball, President Kimball; Elder John Jones, Elder Jones; Presiding Bishop John Jones, Bishop Jones; Bishop Joseph Jones of the Presiding Bishopric, Bishop Jones.

Numbers

In general, in ordinary reading matter, spell out numbers from one through nine; use figures for 10 and above. The same rules apply to the ordinal numbers. Use *first* through *ninth,* then *10th, 11th, 22nd,* etc.

There are exceptions, however. Important ones include:

Use figures for all ages of humans and animals.

5-year-old girl   the girl is 5   a race for 2-year-olds

Use "Big Ten" for the college conference and spell out eleven for a football team, as "the Buckeye eleven."

Write it: No. 1 boy, No. 2 candidate, etc.

In a sentence where you have numbers below 10 and 10 and above, keep the simplest related form. Thus:

The development has 25 five-room houses, 3 ten-room houses and 1 fourteen-room-house.

Don't begin a sentence with a figure. Spell it out or revise the beginning if that is awkward. Thus: Don't write, "275 citizens have volunteered . . ." Do write, "Two hundred and seventy-five citizens have volunteered . . ." or, "A total of 275 citizens have volunteered . . ."

Addresses

Where streets are numbered, write out the ordinal numbers from First through Ninth and use ordinal figures for 10th and above.

550 Fifth Ave.   *16 E. 16th St.*

Abbreviate Avenue, Boulevard, Square, Street and Terrace in numbered addresses. Abbreviations are:

Ave.   Blvd.   Sq.   St.   Ter.

In body copy, except with numbered addresses, do not abbreviate them. Also, never abbreviate Circle, Drive, Road, Lane, Oval, Place, Plaza or Point.

In addresses, use figures for house numbers, apartment numbers, suite numbers and room numbers.

Abbreviate a direction, with a period, when it appears before a street, as *16 E. 16th St.*

Time

In giving clock time, use figures with the abbreviation a.m. or p.m., as 10:30 a.m. It is acceptable to say 10:30 o'clock Monday morning, but newspapers prefer the shorter version because it saves space. Never write 10:30 a.m. Monday morning. Noon and midnight are best expressed as 12 noon and 12 midnight. If it is pertinent to the story to give the time zone, use capitals as: 10:30 a.m. EDT (or EST). If a time zone stands alone in a sentence, without a specific hour, it is spelled out in lower case letters— eastern daylight time, etc.

Miscellaneous

In direct quotations, commas and periods go inside the quotation marks.

"The club's goal is 100 new members," she said, "and we are confident that we will reach it next month."

When a quotation runs longer than a single paragraph, as when you are reporting a speech, quotation marks are used at the beginning of each paragraph but at the end of only the final paragraph of quoted material.

"The club's goal is 100 new members," she said, "and we are confident we will reach it next month.

"We are so certain of this that we already are making plans for welcoming ceremonies five weeks from today."

For a more complete presentation of style rules, check your library for the *Ayer Public Relations and Publicity Style Book,* based on the common style of The Associated Press and United Press International, *The New York Times* and other authorities.

STRAIGHT NEWS RELEASE

                                              FROM: CONTINUING EDUCATION
                                                    (Publicity Contact)
                                                    (Street address)
                                                    (City, State, zip code)
                                                    (Telephone number)

FOR IMMEDIATE RELEASE   (Date)

Anytown's adult education school opened its 1976-77 term last night, (date), with a total of 288 students enrolled in 17 courses at the high school.

The men's cooking course, offered this year for the first time, was the star attraction, with 24 aspiring chefs. There were 22 women in the sewing class, and in the auto shop there was an even number of 11 women and 11 men.

"This is the third year for adult education in Anytown High School," said Dr. Rhodes Scott, high school principal and director of the adult curriculum, "and each year the students appear more dedicated. Partly this is due to the fact that we've added new courses for which a demand developed, and dropped others where interest lagged. All the students are serious about using their time for a good purpose -- they really want to accomplish something."

All the courses offered this year attracted more than the minimum required to justify a class. In languages, the school has both beginning and advanced courses in English, French and Spanish. There are also beginning and advanced classes in typing, shorthand and art. The other courses are woodworking, auto shop, sewing, writing and men's cooking.

#   #   #

FEATURIZED NEWS RELEASE

                                                    FROM: CONTINUING EDUCATION
                                                            (Publicity Contact)
                                                            (Street address)
EXCLUSIVE TO THE ANYTOWN BLADE   (City, State, zip code)
                                                            (Telephone number)
FOR IMMEDIATE RELEASE
                                                            (Date)

       The school bell rang last night, (date), for 288 of the most eager

students Anytown High School may ever have seen pour into its classrooms

as a group.

       It was the opening of the 1976-77 term of Anytown's adult education

school -- and there wasn't an unwilling scholar to be seen.

       Starting in the parking lot, where the action opened:

       Adm. Goodwin Grafton, retired, and Mrs. Grafton were spotted tugging

an antique dresser out of their station wagon. Both are enrolled in wood-

working and knew that the assignment would be to work on their own project.

       "We're going to renovate this old-timer we found up in a barn," Adm.

Grafton explained. "And what better way to renovate it than here at school

where the shop has all the latest tools . . . and there is room to work . . .

and there is expert advice for the asking. And good company, besides."

       Every mother remembers the tearful farewells on the first day of school

when she dropped off a chick at kindergarten. Here there was the reverse --

Grandma chauffeured to class by her 18-year-old grandson in a snappy white

sports car and his parting words: "I'll pick you up promptly at 10 right

over there by that big oak. Don't worry, I'll be there."

                                                            (more)

                                126

Grandma is Mrs. Lafayette Lewis, who is taking advanced Spanish. "I'm planning on spending three months in Spain next summer with my son and family, who live near Madrid," she said. "I want to see as much of the country as I can -- and being a bit familiar with the language will make a lot of difference."

Mrs. Robert Carlson, enrolled in Typing II, said her husband had opened his own business and she thought she could be helpful to him by brushing up on office skills. "The next time around," she said, "I'll go for shorthand."

The men's cooking course, offered this year for the first time, was a star attraction. There were 24 aspiring chefs -- every one of them just a little uncomfortable in his apron but serious about mastering the culinary arts.

"I'd rather be kidded about an apron," one said, "than be kidded again about burnt chicken and overdone steaks when I get going on the outdoor grill."

In the auto shop, there was an opposite story. A woman student who declined to be identified said she was taking the basic mechanic's course because:

"I'm sick and tired of being ripped off. If my car needs a major overhaul, that's a job for an expert, but I'm tired of being charged for little things somebody tells me are big things when they aren't. I want a little know-how to keep these buzzards in their place."

All told, there are 17 courses. In languages, there are beginning and advanced classes in English, French and Spanish. There are beginning and advanced courses in typing, shorthand and art. The other courses are wood-working, auto shop, sewing, writing and men's cooking.

#   #   #

127

Sample Release No. 3   RADIO/TV NEWS RELEASE

                                        FROM: ANYTOWN EDUCATION COUNCIL
                                              (Publicity Contact)
                                              (Street address)
                                              (City, State, zip code)
<u>FOR RELEASE AT (TIME)</u>   (Telephone number)
<u>(DAY), (DATE)</u>
                                              (Date)

A bright young lady in Anytown High School today, (date), became the first

junior student ever to win the prized Acme Systems college scholarship. She

is Kathleen Ann Hart, 16 years old, of (address). The four-year free tuition

award has been made annually by Acme since 1964 to the most promising student

to be graduated each June from Anytown High.

Miss Hart is the daughter of Dr. and Mrs. Warren Hart. She is completing

high school a year early and plans to enroll in Johns Hopkins University next

fall to study medicine. Far from a bookworm, she is a cheerleader, a member

of the high school orchestra and vice president of the student council.

The board of judges who chose Miss Hart for the award consisted of Dr. Irving

Lee, Princeton University; Dr. Clark Blanchard, surgeon and member of the Anytown

Board of Education; Executive Director Evans Siebert (SEE-bert) of the Anytown

Chamber of Commerce; and the Rev. Lawrence Donaldson of St. Luke's Church. A

school assembly award ceremony will be held next Thursday.

                          #   #   #

PUBLIC SERVICE ANNOUNCEMENT
FOR RADIO

FROM: ANYTOWN GARDEN CLUB
      (Publicity Contact)
      (Street address)
      (City, State, zip code)
      (Telephone number)

TREE-PLANTING WEEK
Starting Date: (Day, Date)
Ending Date: (Day, Date)

      (Date)

<u>FOR BROADCAST AT WILL</u>

Time: 20 seconds

Words: 56

Every state has its Arbor Day for tree planting. But here the Anytown
Garden Club believes one day isn't enough for all that needs doing. So it
is sponsoring Tree-Planting Week beginning May 2 (Sunday). Call or visit
the club for expert advice on what <u>you</u> can do. Trees are one of our most
precious possessions.

#   #   #

Sample Release No. 5

FROM: ANYTOWN GARDEN CLUB
        (Publicity Contact)
        (Street address)
        (City, State, zip code)
        (Telephone number)

        (Date)

TREE-PLANTING WEEK

For use (Day, Date)
  through (Day, Date)

Time: 30 seconds

Words: 70

VIDEO	AUDIO
Slide No. _____ (Town Hall Tree)	ANNCR: Drive by Anytown Town Hall and you'll admire the grand old maple gracing the lawn. Everyone does!
Slide No. _____ (Treeless street)	But some parts of Anytown aren't that fortunate in their foliage. To do something about that, the Anytown Garden Club is sponsoring this week as Tree-Planting Week.
Slide No. _____ (Tree-Planting Week May 2-8, 1976) (Blank following "Slide No." is for station to insert its own identifying number on slides you provide.)	During this week, call or visit the club for expert advice on what <u>you</u> can do. Trees are one of our most precious possessions.

#   #   #

130

Sample Release No. 6 SCHOLARSHIP RELEASE

FROM: ANYTOWN EDUCATION COUNCIL
(Publicity Contact)
(Street address)
(City, State, zip code)
(Telephone number)

FOR IMMEDIATE RELEASE (Date)

JUNIOR MISS WINS

ACME SCHOLARSHIP

Kathleen Hart, an advanced junior in Anytown High School, today, (date), won the four-year college scholarship awarded annually by Acme Systems for the most promising student in the June graduating class.

Kathleen, daughter of Dr. and Mrs. Warren Hart, 948 Sheffield Court, is the first junior to win the scholarship since it was established in 1964. She has been studying under a schedule designed to complete the regular four-year high school course in three years. She plans to pursue her education studying medicine at Johns Hopkins University, Baltimore, MD.

Board Chairman Brian Mitchell of Acme, a pioneering firm in space-age technology, said in announcing the award:

"Kathleen Hart astounded our board of judges with her maturity, her intelligence, her all-around ability and her dedicated approach to a medical career. We are engineers, but we respect the world of medicine. We are honored to have such an outstanding young lady receive the award."

(more)

Far from a bookworm, Kathleen is a member of the Anytown High
School orchestra, playing the cello; a cheerleader for football,
basketball and baseball; and vice president of the student council.
She is a good swimmer and works hard in her spare time at becoming
a gourmet cook.

Her parents have resided in Anytown for 25 years, ever since
Dr. Hart joined United Polymers in Wallingford as chief chemist.

The scholarship will be awarded formally by Mr. Mitchell next
Tuesday, (date), at a school assembly ceremony. Acme, a firm specializing in strategic systems, high-energy lasers and space-age assemblies,
has been awarding four-year college scholarships since 1964 because, in
the words of Mr. Mitchell, "our young people are our tomorrow."

The Acme board of judges is composed of Dr. Irving Lee, dean of the
communications school at Princeton University; Dr. Clark Blanchard,
surgeon and member of the Anytown Board of Education; Evans Siebert,
Chamber of Commerce executive director; and the Rev. Lawrence Donaldson
of St. Luke's Church.

Previous winners of the award include Dr. Steven Scott, who was a
local student who became a Rhodes Scholar and now is a practicing
physician; the well-known television personality, Harvey Burton; and
Arnold Randolph, the Anytown Hills architect.

# # #

Sample Release No. 7   ENGAGEMENT RELEASE

                                          FROM: (Publicity Contact)
                                                 (Street address)
                                                 (City, State, zip code)
ATTENTION: SOCIETY EDITOR   (Telephone number)

FOR IMMEDIATE RELEASE   (Date)

     Mr. and Mrs. Robert Westlake of 110 Walton Road have announced the

engagement of their daughter, Frances, to Randolph Collison, son of Mr.

and Mrs. William Collison of 375 Granada Blvd.

     (Another situation: Mr. and Mrs. Robert Westlake of 110 Walton

Road have announced the engagement of their daughter, Frances, to Ran-

dolph Collison, son of Mrs. William Collison of 375 Granada Blvd. and

the late Mr. Collison.)

     (Another situation: Mr. and Mrs. Robert Westlake of 110 Walton

Road have announced the engagement of their daughter, Frances, to Ran-

dolph Collison, son of William Collison of Black Rock, CT., and Mrs.

Harry Rhodes of Tampa, FL.)

     Miss Westlake is a graduate of Anytown High School and the Uni-

versity of Illinois, where she majored in home economics. She is a

home economist in the food center of Warren & O'Connor, New York ad-

vertising agency.

     Mr. Collison also was graduated from Anytown High School; served four

years in the U. S. Navy, including one year in Saigon; and was graduated

last year from the University of California, where he majored in marketing.

He is with Acme Systems as a marketing specialist.

     A September 30 wedding is planned.

                         #   #   #

Sample Release No. 8   WEDDING RELEASE

FROM: (Publicity Contact)
        (Street address)
        (City, State, zip code)
ATTENTION: SOCIETY EDITOR   (Telephone number)

FOR IMMEDIATE RELEASE   (Date)

Miss Frances Westlake, daughter of Mr. and Mrs. Robert Westlake of 110 Walton Road, became the bride of Randolph Collison, son of Mr. and Mrs. William Collison of 375 Granada Blvd., at an 11:30 a.m. ceremony today, (date), in the St. Paul's Chapel of Columbus College.

The Rev. Dr. Steven Denison of the Broadway Presbyterian Church in New York, a friend of the couple for many years, officiated. He was assisted by the Rev. Huntington Evans of St. Paul's.

Miss Linda Evans Westlake, sister of the bride, was maid of honor. Other attendants were Emelie Lewis, Kathy Jolly and Leslie George, who was flower girl. The best man was Scott Hart and the ushers were Howard Tower and Gil Hart. The wedding was followed by a reception at the Pelham Yacht Club.

Mrs. Westlake is a home economist with Warren & O'Connor, New York advertising agency. She is a graduate of Anytown High School and the University of Illinois. Mr. Collison also is a graduate of Anytown High. After naval service, he was graduated from the University of California in marketing and now is a marketing specialist with Acme Systems.

(Now, depending on what your publications use, you can follow with details about the parents or grandparents of the bride and/or groom, if they are notable, and/or you can describe what the bride and her attendants

(more)

134

(page 2 - Westlake wedding)

wore. As follows.)

The bride wore an ivory satin gown with a small train. The silk il-
lusion bouffant veil was edged with Alençon lace and fell from a crown of
ivory silk satin covered with lace and pearls. She carried a bouquet
of gardenias.

The bride's sister as maid of honor wore a mint green jersey halter
gown with an emerald green velvet jacket. A small band of baby's breath
was worn for a headdress.

The bridesmaids each wore a jersey halter gown, Miss Lewis in pink
with a ruby velvet jacket; Miss Jolly in sky blue and royal blue velvet;
and Miss George in a lavender dress and a berry velvet jacket. The headdress
of each bridesmaid was a small band of baby's breath.

Mr. and Mrs. Collison left for a two-week honeymoon in the Canary Islands.
They will live in Anytown upon their return.

(Note: If there is anything different about the wedding with respect to
music, or the ceremony -- such as the Greek Orthodox custom of crossing
crowns of white flowers over the heads of the couple, or the crossing
of swords for a military ceremony -- be sure to bring that in well up at
the top. Recognize that many wedding ceremonies read alike -- so anything
that is different, that varies from the conventional, should be mentioned
or accented. Young people today are very innovative in the ceremony,
very creative, so make the most in your stories of what is interesting
and different.)

#   #   #

135

Sample Release No. 9

FROM: ANYTOWN COMMUNITY ASS'N
          (Publicity contact)
          (Street address)
          (City, State, zip code)
          (Telephone number)

<u>FOR IMMEDIATE RELEASE</u>   (Date)

Mrs. Robert Hawthorne was elected president of the Anytown Community Association for 1976-77 today, (date), by the board of governors at its annual special election session at the ACA clubhouse.

Other officers chosen by the board were: Mrs. Frank Newton, first vice president; Mrs. Hamilton Fenton, second vice president; Mrs. William Jewett, reelected secretary; and Mrs. John Wright, reelected treasurer.

Mrs. Hawthorne, a vice president for four terms and active on ACA committees for 15 years, succeeds Mrs. Bruce Price. Mrs. Price, who has been president for five terms, now joins the board of governors.

The new administration will be installed at a members tea to be held at 4 o'clock Saturday afternoon, (date), in the clubhouse.

(For a small organization with limited community activity, this brief release may suffice. For a larger organization engaged in many community programs, however, a release of this type should be amplified with interesting details about the officers, highlights of the outgoing president's achievements, membership growth, etc. Give street addresses for the officers if your outlets customarily use them.)

# # #

Sample Release No. 10   DEMONSTRATION RELEASE

                                         FROM: CUB PACK 25
                                                (Publicity Contact)
                                                (Street address)
                                                (City, State, zip code)
                                                (Telephone number)

FOR IMMEDIATE RELEASE   (Date)

        A demonstration of knot tying for amateurs with as varied inter-

ests as sailing, fishing or the safe delivery of a gift parcel will be

presented at 7:30 p.m. next Tuesday, (date), in the Anytown High School

auditorium under auspices of Cub Pack 25.

        Charles Seaton, noted yachtsman and outdoor writer, whose son,

Charles Jr., is a member of the pack, will conduct the slide-illus-

trated demonstration. The public is invited.

        "This program is being offered as our way of thanking the commu-

nity for its support," said Cubmaster Fred McKay.

        "Mr. Seaton makes working with knots a lot of fun -- but fun with a

purpose, whether you want to know the right way to fasten a tow rope

to your car, the basic knots you need in boating or how to tie nylon

fishing line so it will hold. And a lot more, too.

        "Everyone is welcome, but one suggestion: Bring along a couple of

short lengths of sash cord or clothes line and learn by doing. Along with

the useful knots there'll be some parlor tricks everyone will enjoy."

                            #   #   #

Sample Release No. 11   ACHIEVEMENT NEWS RELEASE

FROM: ANYTOWN WOMEN'S CLUB
        (Publicity Contact)
        (Street address)
        (City, State, zip code)
        (Telephone number)

FOR IMMEDIATE RELEASE   (Date)

Mrs. Kenneth Curtis of 111 Beach Drive was chosen "Community Woman of
the Year" today, (date), by the Joint Honors Committee of the Anytown Women's
Club and the Anytown Business and Professional Women's Association for her
outstanding service to the community.

The committee, at a special meeting at the Women's Club, cited Mrs. Curtis
for "not one but two distinguished achievements" -- her leadership in
establishing a garden club for youngsters and her conduct of the Minigarden Beautification Program in Anytown's business section.

Mrs. Curtis, a member of the Anytown Garden Club for 20 years and its
president for five terms, is the first woman outside of the organizations
represented on the Joint Honors Committee to win the award.

Under the Junior Garden Club founded by her, junior and senior high school
students are given instruction on vegetable and flower gardens, shrubs and trees.
These are short courses designed to make gardening rewarding fun. Each year
since the program began four years ago the number of students has grown. A
record 325 enrolled this year.

Under the Minigarden Beautification Program, also initiated by Mrs. Curtis,
there now are 17 natural beautification projects in the downtown business and
railroad sections of the city which have turned town eyesores into garden
beauty spots.

A scroll and $1,000 check to forward these projects will be formally presented
to Mrs. Curtis Friday, (date), at an Honors Banquet.

#   #   #

Sample Release No. 12

FROM: ANYTOWN BOAT CLUB
        (Publicity Contact)
        (Street address)
        (City, State, zip code)
        (Telephone number)

FOR IMMEDIATE RELEASE   (Date)

National Safe Boating Week, which starts next Sunday, (date), will be
marked locally with a series of daily safe boating demonstrations by members
of the Anytown Boat Club at the club's main dock at Pear Tree Point.

Under the schedule announced today by the club, there will be free public
demonstrations every half hour from 2 p.m. to 6 p.m. Sunday; at 10 o'clock
each morning and at 4 o'clock each afternoon every week day; and every half
hour from 2 p.m. to 6 p.m. on the final day.

Rear Adm. Spencer X. Ferguson, retired, head of the club, said: "Pleasure
boating should be just that -- pleasure for all. Though fatalities nationally
are at an all-time low, they're higher than they would be if everyone who step-
ped into a boat had some basic training and used his head. We always face
the problem that accidents may go higher as more people, with more recreation
time on their hands, turn to boating.

"We can't make safe sailors out of nonsailors by a single demonstration, but
we can expose new boatowners, prospective boatowners and the vacationers who get
to the water just once a year to some fundamental safety rules."

Plans are being formulated by the club to offer a free safety training
course next fall or winter. Details are expected to be announced after Labor Day.

#   #   #

Sample Release No. 13   CONVENTION DELEGATES

                                        FROM: LEAGUE OF WOMEN VOTERS
                                               (Publicity Contact)
                                               (Street address)
                                               (City, State, zip code)

FOR IMMEDIATE RELEASE   (Date)

        The Anytown League of Women Voters will send five delegates to the 36th

state convention of the league, to be held, (date), at (State) Central College,

(city).

        Some 250 delegates from 63 local leagues are expected to attend the two-

day sessions, which will debate and adopt the state program for the next two

years, elect officers and directors, and adopt a budget.

        The proposed program, distilled from suggestions made by league members

throughout the state, focuses on four main areas -- tax reform, a balanced trans-

portation system, representative government and environmental quality.

        (When a local organization actually instructs its delegates how to vote at

a convention, this should be in the first paragraph if it is an issue of public

interest, and the reasons explained in the body of the story.)

        The Anytown delegates are:

        (In giving their names, follow organization practice or individual prefer-

ences. A married woman may choose in some organization work to use her husband's

name, prefaced by Mrs. Or she may choose to use Mrs., her first name and her

husband's last name. Or she may drop the Mrs. and use her first name and her

husband's last name. Street addresses may or may not be given. Here the pref-

erences of the newspapers receiving the release should be your guide.)

        (A release such as this should be amplified with highlights of the con-

vention program -- keynote speaker, banquet program, etc.)

                                #   #   #

                                      140

Sample Release No. 14   COMMUNITY SERVICE RELEASE

                                         FROM: ANYTOWN BOAT CLUB
                                                 (Publicity Contact)
                                                 (Street address)
                                                 (City, State, zip code)
                                                 (Telephone number)

<u>FOR IMMEDIATE RELEASE</u>   (Date)

     A 10-week free course on the basics of safe boating will be offered

to the community by the Anytown Boat Club, beginning at 8 o'clock next

Tuesday night, (date), in the Anytown High School.

     Registration will take place the first night of the course, which will

continue on Tuesday nights through (date). It is not necessary to be a boatowner

to enroll. Minimum age is 15 years.

     "The course will emphasize the proper operation of all types of boats,

especially the family outboard," said Rear Adm. Spencer X. Ferguson, retired,

the club's commander. "Classes will be taught by our members, who are volun-

teering their time and effort and experience to promote boating safety.

     "Anyone who goes out on the water without proper knowledge of the rules

of the road, safety requirements and aids to navigation is asking for trouble.

With the information offered in this free course, a boater will have the

minimum knowledge for safe boating and be confident of being able to cope with

the many situations one may face."

     Subjects to be covered include boat handling under normal and adverse

conditions, seamanship and common emergencies, rules of the road, aids to

navigation, compass and chart familiarization, running lights and equipment,

boat trailering and river boating.

                                                            (more)

(page 2 - boating course)

   "Our course lays a basic foundation for building boating skills
through further study, application and experience," Rear Adm. Ferguson
added.

   "We regret that we had to establish a minimum age of 15 years for this
course, but it was necessary to keep the classes to working size. However,
we recognize the very great need to begin boating training at an earlier
age. Hence, next spring, we plan another course for youngsters."

                              #   #   #

Sample Release No. 15   NEW FACILITIES RELEASE

                                        FROM: ANYTOWN COMMUNITY HOSPITAL
                                                 (Publicity Contact)
                                                 (Street address)
                                                 (City, State, zip code)
                                                 (Telephone number)

FOR IMMEDIATE RELEASE   (Date)

        Ground-breaking ceremonies for Blake Pavilion, the third major unit in

the Anytown Community Hospital's $23.7 million expansion program, will be held

at 11 a.m. Saturday, (date), at the construction site behind the hospital on

North Street.

        David Barber, chairman of the board of trustees, announced that the first

symbolic spadeful of earth would be turned by Mrs. R. Edmund Blake, widow of the

man honored by the name of the facility for his 35 years of leadership in the

hospital's development.

        There will be a brief program with national, state and local officials

participating. Program details will be announced next week. An open invi-

tation to attend has been extended to the community.

        The ground breaking is for a five-story structure providing a total of

266,000 square feet of space for a new ambulatory service, including an ambula-

tory surgery center, emergency department and facilities for first encounter,

testing and patient evaluation. It will include also enlarged and modernized

facilities for specialty and sub-specialty diagnostic treatment services.

There will be space for public areas, support services and administrative of-

fices. The top two floors will be devoted to rooms for patients.

                                                          (more)

Blake Pavilion will be situated behind the present main hospital building, between the southeast wing and the old School of Nursing Building. Access will be provided both from North Street and Prospect Street. The pavilion will be connected with the main hospital building by both ground-floor and first-floor walkways with window walls allowing full views of gardens on both sides.

Previously, in the expansion program, a new medical records department had been completed, going into operation last March. A new laundry is under construction and scheduled to go into operation late next month. Blake Pavilion is scheduled for completion next summer.

Architects for Blake Pavilion were the local firm of Richard Z. Nelson Associates, working in conjunction with a Baltimore firm specializing in hospital architecture, Institutional Ambience Architects, Inc. The construction bid was let last month to the local firm of Rondano Brothers and Murtz.

#   #   #

Accompanying material:

Architect's sketch, Blake Pavilion
Site location map.

ORGANIZATION ANNIVERSARY

                              FROM: ANYTOWN GARDEN CLUB
                                     (Publicity contact)
                                     (Street address)
                                     (City, State, zip code)
                                     (Telephone number)

FOR IMMEDIATE RELEASE   (Date)

                    (Straight News Approach)

An eight-day program of community events to celebrate the 50th anni-

versary of the Anytown Garden Club, beginning with the planting of 50

trees on Saturday, (date), as the club's birthday present to Anytown, was

announced today.

                    (Featurized Approach)

Rain or shine, Anytown is going to get a special birthday gift of 50

trees, planted where they're needed the most, on Saturday, (date).

It's not Anytown's birthday, but the opening event in an eight-day

celebration of the 50th anniversary of the Anytown Garden Club.

                (Story continues from either lead)

Other activities in the program announced by the club's Golden

Anniversary Committee, headed by Mrs. Gordon Graham, the club's presi-

dent, include:

   --Open house at the organization's Hawthorne Lane clubhouse and gardens

   every day from 2 p.m. to 9 p.m. from Sunday, (date), through

   Friday, (date). Features will be a flower show and, from 2 to

   4 p.m. Sunday and 5:30 to 8 p.m. weekdays there will be Quiz Me booths

   staffed with experts to answer visitors' gardening questions.

                                        (more)

--Announcement on Monday, (date), at a high school assembly of the
club's first Green Thumb Award, to be given annually to the high
school student judged to have shown the greatest leadership and
gardening curiosity in the program of the Junior Garden Club. Besides a plaque, the winner will receive a $500 college scholarship
award.

--A banquet at 7 p.m. Saturday, (date), at the Civic Center, followed
by a public presentation on "How to Be a Lazy Gardener -- Yet Get
Results" by Fred Wallingford, noted author, TV personality and
gardening enthusiast. As a curtain raiser to this program in the
Auditorium, the men members of the club will present a "This Is
Your Life" review of the club's 50 years. Special guests will be
senior citizens responsible for taking care of the club's 20 Minigardens beautifying the downtown and outlying shopping centers,
the railroad station grounds and the schools.

A special subgroup of the Golden Anniversary Committee has been working
for three months on selecting sites for the 50 trees to be planted for the
greatest community benefit. Among the prominent bare spots to be filled are
the front lawn of the Town Hall, which lost two graceful elms to Dutch elm
disease a number of years ago; the Public Library yard, whose prize maple lost
the battle with last winter's ice storm; and the once-neglected weed patch
marking the entry way to the railroad station, now beautified under care of the
Senior Citizen Garden Club group but to be enhanced by three dwarf evergreens.

The Golden Anniversary Committee has recruited a task force of

(more)

146

men club members and publicly spirited citizens, high school students
and Junior and Senior Citizen Garden Club members to do the actual
planting. A map showing the tree-planting sites will be published
a week from today in the Anytown Blade.

"In picking the trees to be planted," Mrs. Graham explained, "we
were guided generally by the specific requirements of each site. If a
maple was needed to balance a maple, that's what we chose. The 50 trees
are maples, oaks, pink dogwood, white dogwood, and a variety of evergreens. For the most prominent spots, we obtained the most mature
specimens we could handle so that the community can begin enjoying them
at once."

"The Quiz Me booths at the daily open houses could be a lot of fun,"
she added, "for not only do we expect people with indoor or outdoor garden problems and questions to come in for advice, but we do hope that
those who have worked out their own home remedies will give us the benefit of their successes."

The concluding event of the birthday celebration, Fred Wallingford's illustrated presentation on "How to Be a Lazy Gardener - Yet Get
Results," will be at 9:15 p.m. Saturday, (date), in the Civic Center
Auditorium, and will be open to the public. Free tickets, as long as
the supply lasts, may be obtained at the clubhouse or from any member.

(Here, proceed with a short history of the club -- who founded it and
why; its noteworthy accomplishments in its 50 years; who the principal
forces have been in its development; its presidents; its headquarters.)

#   #   #

COMBINING SPEECH, BANQUET
AND COMMUNITY SERVICE

FROM: ANYTOWN GARDEN CLUB
        (Publicity contact)
        (Street address)
        (City, State, zip code)
        (Telephone number)

FOR IMMEDIATE RELEASE

(Date)

A new program for bringing young people and the elderly together through gardening was announced last night, (date), at the annual supper-meeting of the Anytown Garden Club by Mrs. Gordon Graham, club president.

The buffet supper in the Civic Center was organized by the men members of the club and attracted more than 800 members. Mrs. Graham spoke in the Civic Center auditorium after the supper.

"Our new program, which we have named 'Green Chums,'" Mrs. Graham said, "is designed to contribute to the growing nationwide recognition of the importance of keeping the elderly actively participating in some purposeful effort.

"We are aware of the number of organized activities by clubs for the retired, but we are aware also of the fact that some people don't like group activities and others, incapacitated, can't participate. All of us have heard over and over again about the generation gap, and we are persuaded that when generations draw apart, both young people and the elderly are deprived of important values.

"Our Green Chum program is a new experiment attempting to do something about the problem in ways that will benefit everyone. Basically, members of our Junior Garden Club will work on various garden projects with retired people."

(more)

For shut-ins, she explained, there will be window-sill projects. For apartment dwellers, there will not only be window-sill and balcony projects, but for those interested in outside gardening there will be cooperative plots to be planned and tilled in association with Junior Garden Club members.

"And for those who have their own gardens, but shy away from the normal organized activities for the retired," Mrs. Graham continued, "we believe we have a remedy for their loneliness by having one or more Junior Garden Club members work with them.

"This is no one-way street," she pointed out. "The juniors will benefit from the experience. We have talked it over very seriously with them in developing this program, and we have been overwhelmed by their enthusiastic response.

"Frankly, we checked them out first, because their energy and their enthusiasm are essential ingredients. But we also checked out a number of the retired -- and again the response was overwhelming."

A special Green Chums committee has been appointed, with Mrs. Douglas Saxton as chairwoman and two members of the Junior Garden Club as vice chairpersons, Judy Burns and Harold Mitchell. Additional information about the program for those interested in participating may be obtained from Mrs. Saxton at the club headquarters.

Mrs. Graham said the idea for the program came from an experiment in green therapy she read about in New Jersey that had had excellent success with shut-ins.

#   #   #

FROM: ANYTOWN HISTORICAL SOCIETY
       (Publicity contact)
       (Street address)
       (City, State, zip code)
       (Telephone number)

FOR IMMEDIATE RELEASE
(Date)

The Anytown Historical Society's fifth annual holiday exhibition, to be on display throughout December, will present "Anytown Through the Years" as captured by local artists in oils, water colors and needlepoint.

Town House, the society's headquarters, will be open for the exhibition weekdays from 10 a.m. to 5 p.m., and on Saturdays and Sundays from 2 p.m. to 8 p.m. It will be closed Christmas Day.

The society's traditional Christmas Sing will be held on the Sunday before Christmas, (date), at 4 p.m. in the main exhibition room.

"This is the most exciting exhibition we have ever arranged," said Mrs. Lincoln Dunlap, president. "Not only will we have on loan the prized possessions now hanging in many private homes, but we have uncovered many treasures hidden away in attics.

"Most unusual are the number of fine needlepoint works we shall show, including a local scene sketched 110 years ago by a 10-year-old girl and later transferred in enlarged form into a needlepoint pattern."

Each exhibit will be provided with an explanatory background, and in some cases where a scene is pictured there will be a modern-day photograph of the same scene.

#   #   #

Sample Release No. 19   COMMITTEE APPOINTMENTS

                                        FROM: ANYTOWN COMMUNITY ASS'N
                                                (Publicity contact)
                                                (Street address)
                                                (City, State, zip code)
                                                (Telephone number)

<u>FOR IMMEDIATE RELEASE</u>   (Date)

        Mrs. Robert Hawthorne, president of the Anytown Community Association,

today, (date), named 15 committee chairwomen and 15 vice chairwomen to conduct

the association's programs and activities in the coming year.

        The general committee, composed of the chairwomen of all committees, will

be headed by Mrs. Frank Newton, first vice president. Vice chairwoman is Mrs.

Carl Hoyt.

        Chairwoman of community activities is the second vice president, Mrs. Hamil-

ton Fenton. Vice chairwoman is Mrs. Marshall Moore.

        Other appointments were:

        Steering committee -- Mrs. David Williams, chairwoman; Mrs. Stanley Easton,

vice chairwoman.

        Membership -- Mrs. Russell King, chairwoman; Mrs. Arthur Davis, vice chair-

woman.

        Program -- Mrs. Stewart Sawyer, chairwoman; Mrs. David Cameron, vice chair-

woman.

        Community Liaison -- Mrs. Lincoln Dunlap, chairwoman; Mrs. Paul Kingman,

vice chairwoman.

        Philanthropic Activities -- Mrs. Frances Hughes, chairwoman; Mrs. Ramsay

Knapp, vice chairwoman.

                                                        (more)

                                151

Scholarship -- Mrs. Gordon Graham, chairwoman; Mrs. Lawrence Crawford, vice chairwoman.

60-Plus Club -- Mrs. Philip A. Taylor, chairwoman; Mrs. Fred Hughes Jr., vice chairwoman.

Arts and Crafts -- Mrs. Bradford Clark, chairwoman; Mrs. James Baker, vice chairwoman.

Open House and Fair -- Mrs. Parker Craig, chairwoman; Mrs. Robert Snyder, vice chairwoman.

Nominating -- Mrs. Harold M. Rich, chairwoman; Mrs. John Vance, vice chair-woman.

Clubhouse and Gardens -- Mrs. Warren H. Wagner, chairwoman; Mrs. Sylvester Reed, vice chairwoman.

Archives -- Mrs. Bruce Price, former president, chairwoman; Mrs. Hoyt Scofield, vice chairwoman.

Publicity -- Mrs. Charles Davies, chairwoman; Mrs. Kent Atwood, vice chair-woman.

Mrs. Hawthorne has asked the committee chairwomen to complete their com-mittees in two weeks for presentation to the board of governors. The com-mittees with programs to develop are to have their projects fully mapped out for approval and announcement to the membership by mid-August.

(Include addresses of all appointees if your media outlets use addresses.)

# # #

152

FUND-RAISING BENEFIT

                                            FROM: ANYTOWN DAY CARE
                                                    (Publicity contact)
                                                    (Street address)
                                                    (City, State, zip code)
                                                    (Telephone number)

FOR IMMEDIATE RELEASE   (Date)

     The annual house and garden tour for the benefit of the Anytown day care

centers will be held Saturday, (date), featuring 10 private homes and gardens

of unusual interest, Mrs. Theodore Paxton, general chairwoman, announced

today, (date).

     Tour hours will be from 11 a.m. to 6 p.m. Tickets will be available

at all day care centers and at special tables at all banks and the railroad

station for two weeks before the tour. A buffet luncheon, for which tickets

must be purchased no later than a day in advance at the same places tour

tickets will be available, will be served at the Ridgeway Day Care Center

from 12 noon to 2 p.m. on tour day.

     Houses on the tour will range from Anytown's oldest private home, Blan-

chard House, to the newly completed ultra-modern home of the renowned archi-

tect, Curtis Bradford, and Mrs. Bradford on Pasture Lane.

     Gardens will include the rose garden at the Fred Wallingford home, the

formal English garden at the Clark Thomas home, the Japanese Garden at the

David Brophy home, and the extensive herb gardens developed originally by the

great-grandparents of Robert Hawthorne at the ancestral Hawthorne home.

                                                         (more)

In the center of town, the old Loftis mansion next to the Public Library has been renovated with great care by Mr. and Mrs. David Richardson and will be open on the tour for the first time. Other homes new to the tour are the white colonial of Mr. and Mrs. Wallace Sawyer; the Civil War brick of Mr. and Mrs. George Davies; and, out in the country, the Robert Allen homestead.

Serving with Mrs. Paxton as co-chairwomen of the special committee sponsoring the benefit are Mrs. Gordon Crouse, Mrs. Carl Hoyt, Mrs. Hamilton Fenton, and Mrs. Ramsay Knapp.

Proceeds from the tour and buffet luncheon will go toward the support of Anytown's five day care centers. These started 10 years ago as places where working mothers could leave their children. They were, in effect, baby-sitting services. In recent years, however, programs have been developed to give the youngsters significant educational and cultural opportunities. Among other things, there are arts and crafts workshops and tutorial programs for under-achievers.

This will be the fifth annual tour sponsored by a special committee. Last year, more than 1,200 visitors participated.

The tour has the support of the Anytown Council of Churches, which is sponsoring the buffet luncheon through a group kitchen committee headed by Mrs. Lawrence Donaldson.

A map showing all the houses and gardens on the tour will be provided to each ticket purchaser.

#   #   #

FROM: ACME SYSTEMS, INC.
        (Publicity Contact)
        (Street address)
        (City, State, zip code)
ATTENTION: BUSINESS NEWS EDITOR   (Telephone number)

FOR IMMEDIATE RELEASE   (Date)

Peter Jolly of 666 Fairview Ave. was elected president of Acme Systems, Inc., today, (date), at a special meeting of the board of directors. He succeeded the late George Slocum.

Brian Mitchell continues as chairman of the board, but other new officers were elected as follows:

Robert Westlake of 110 Walton Road to succeed Mr. Jolly as executive vice president; Harry Walmsley of 530 Oconomowac Drive to succeed Mr. Westlake as vice president of operations; and Lewis Kelly, formerly with Trident Manufacturing, Geneva, IL., to fill Mr. Westlake's former post as general manager.

Mr. Jolly, who was born and raised in Anytown, started with Acme as an office boy 35 years ago. He left after two years to attend the Ken School of Business Administration and returned to Acme after earning his degree. He has been responsible for many of the company's innovations in marketing.

(For a local release, this story could proceed with the careers of each of the other new officers, after completing details of Mr. Jolly's business and community activities. For a trade magazine release, omit the local activities but define Acme Systems briefly. Keep it simple; keep it short.)

#   #   #

ORGANIZATION FACT SHEET

FROM: ANYTOWN GARDEN CLUB
        (Publicity Contact)
        (Street address)
        (City, State, zip code)
        (Telephone number)

        (Date)

FACT SHEET

ANYTOWN GARDEN CLUB

EARLY YEARS . . . Founded in the spring of 1926 by Amy Watson (the late Mrs.
Fred H. Everett) and Helen Knapp (Mrs. Gordon Graham, the
current president).

As high-school students in World War I, the co-founders
first became interested in gardening through the War Gardens students planted in community plots where the present
high school now stands. Both returned to Anytown from college. Finding a small group of gardening enthusiasts among
their friends, they decided to form the Anytown Garden Club.

In the beginning, the club met once a month in members' homes.
Flower arranging was the principal activity. In 1932, the
club staged its first flower show. Flower shows now are
twice-a-year major events -- in spring and fall.

CLUB HOUSE. . . A giant step forward in the club's development was taken in
1934 when the late Emory Watson, father of Amy Watson, left
his mansion and five-acre estate to the club for its headquarters. Members contributed their time and money to con-
vert the home into a working headquarters facility and to
improve and enlarge the existing gardens.

In 1941, when the five acres behind the estate went on the
market, the club raised a fund to buy the property. It since
has been developed into a variety of special gardens and provides plots for Junior Garden Club members and other projects,
as well as parking.

MEMBERSHIP . . . More than 500 families and 400 individuals have memberships.
The Junior Garden Club comprises 100 members. The basic
qualification is an interest in some facet of gardening.

HEADQUARTERS . . Clubhouse, at 115 Pasture Lane, is open weekdays, 10 a.m.-
5 p.m.; Saturdays, 10 a.m.-12 noon. Gardens open to public
during same hours. Headquarters telephone: (number).

ACTIVITIES . . . Regular programs include workshops and lectures on outdoor
and indoor gardening by member-specialists or outside experts, and demonstrations of flower arranging. Many are open
to the public.

There are regular competitions in flower arranging and for
flower and vegetable growers.

The Spring Flower Show is held annually in mid-May; the
Fall Flower Show is held annually, usually the third week of
September.

The Junior Garden Club for youngsters through high-school age
was established in 1965. Garden plots at Headquarters provide
experimental and showplace sites. Lectures and workshops.

Green Thumb Award established in 1976. Plaque and $500 col-
lege scholarship awarded to Junior Garden Club high school
senior for gardening interest and leadership.

Minigarden program to beautify town spots launched in 1970.
Fifteen Minigardens established and maintained in formerly
neglected sites.

"Green Chums" program to bring youngsters and oldsters together through gardening established in 1976.

OFFICERS . . . . President, Mrs. Gordon Graham, (address) (phone number);
Vice Presidents, Mr. and Mrs. David Richardson, (address)
   (phone number);
Membership Chairwoman, Mrs. Charles Hartley, (address)
   (phone number);
Secretary, Mrs. Alfred W. Stillman, (address) (phone number);
Treasurer, Charles Collings, (address) (phone number);
Publicity, Mrs. Grant Rose, (address) (phone number at Head-
   quarters and at home, or wherever else reachable);
Junior Garden Club, Directors, Judy Burns, (address) (phone
   number), and Harold Mitchell, (address) (phone number);
Special Projects Coordinator (Green Chums and Minigarden
   programs), Mrs. William J. Bach, (address) (phone number).

FOR ADDITIONAL
INFORMATION . .   General, telephone Headquarters (phone number), 10 a.m.-
5 p.m. weekdays, 10 a.m.-12 noon, Saturdays. Publicity,
call Mrs. Rose (phone number and time available) and
(phone number after hours).

　　　　　　　　ANNIVERSARY FACT SHEET

FROM:　ANYTOWN GARDEN CLUB
　　　　(Publicity Contact)
　　　　(Street address)
　　　　(City, State, zip code)
　　　　(Telephone number)

(Date)

FACT SHEET ON

GOLDEN ANNIVERSARY CELEBRATION, ANYTOWN GARDEN CLUB

WHEN -- Saturday, (date), through Saturday, (date).

WHAT -- Five community events --

* Fifty trees to be planted, (date), as club's gift to Anytown.

* Daily open houses, Sunday, (date), through Friday, (date), at
Hawthorne Lane clubhouse and gardens, featuring flower show
and Quiz Me booths where experts will answer visitors'
gardening questions. Open house hours -- 2 to 9 p.m. daily;
Quiz Me booths -- 2-4 p.m. Sunday and 5:30 to 8 p.m. weekdays.

* First Green Thumb Award ceremony, 1 p.m. Monday, (date), at
special high school assembly, for Junior Garden Club winner
of plaque for gardening interest and leadership, and $500
college scholarship.

* Members' banquet, 7 p.m. Saturday, (date), Civic Center.
Special guests will be senior citizens who take care of the
club-sponsored Minigardens beautifying 20 spots in Anytown.

* Post-banquet program, open by free tickets to the public.
9:15 p.m., (date), Civic Center Auditorium, featuring a short
"This Is Your Life" skit on the club's 50 years and an illustrated presentation on "How to Be a Lazy Gardener -- Yet Get
Results" by Fred Wallingford, author, TV personality and prize
amateur gardener.

COMMITTEES -- Golden Anniversary Committee, chairwoman, Mrs. Gordon
Graham, president, Anytown Garden Club. Tree Planting Project
Committee, co-chaired by Mrs. Bruce Biefielden and Mrs. Lindley
Thompson. Open House Committee, Mrs. Jerome Windsor, chairwoman;
Flower Show organized by Mr. and Mrs. Wayne Watson and Mr. and
Mrs. Arthur Davis; Quiz Me Booths conducted by Dr. and Mrs. David
Williams. Banquet and Program Committee, chairman, Howard Richardson.

FOR FURTHER INFORMATION -- Call (publicity contact) (telephone number).

# # #